D0230266

Contents

Dedication

To the memory of Samuel Sheldon (1918–1999), loving father, lifelong socialist, and a soldier of the Second World War, and to the memory of Nagaretnun Shanmuganathan (1931–1995), devoted father, gifted teacher, and passionate advocate of education for all.

About the Authors

Brian Sheldon (PhD, MPhil, DipSS, DipPSW, RMN, Registered Psycotherapist) is Professor of Applied Social Research, and Director of the Centre for Evidence-based Social Services at the University of Exeter (UK). He has had a long-standing interest in research on the effectiveness of Social Services and has contributed many articles and books to the literature on this subject. The project (CEBSS) of which he is Director has recently been re-funded for a further 3 years by the Department of Health and the regional consortium of sixteen Social Services departments.

Rupatharshini Chilvers (Reseach Assistant in CEBSS) holds a degree in Psychology from the University of Wales (Bangor) and an MSc in Psychological Research Methods from the University of Exeter. Her main interets lie in health and social care research, and in electronic dissemination methods.

Acknowledgements

The authors wish to extend their thanks to Sue Bosely, Alice Caldwell and Annie Ellis (present and past members of the Centre for Evidence-based Social Services), and to Professor Geraldine Macdonald (University of Bristol) for their help and encouragement; friends all as well as colleagues. Thanks also to all those colleagues in social services departments who somehow found time to supply us with the information on which this book is based. Brian Sheldon's daughter Sally Millington produced the index and checked the tables, but she already knows what he thinks of her.

Abbreviations and Specialist Terms

ADSS — *Association of Directors of Social Services.*
BASW — *British Association of Social Workers.*
χ^2 — *Chi square—a test of statistical significance to establish the chances that an association is not due to chance factors alone, e.g. one in a hundred or five in a hundred (p<0.01 and p<0.05, respectively).*
CAMHS — *Child and Adolescent Mental Health Project.*
CASP — *Critical Appraisal Skills Project, Oxford.*
CCETSW — *The Central Council for Education and Training in Social Work.*
CEBSS — *Centre for Evidence-based Social Services, University of Exeter.*
CQSW — *Certificate of Qualification in Social Work—the previous professional qualification in the UK.*
CRD — *Centre for Reviews and Dissemination, University of York*
CSS — *Certificate in Social Services.*
SD — *Standard deviation—a measure of the spread of scores or values from the mean or average.*
DipCOT — *Diploma of the College of Occupational Therapy.*
DipSW — *Diploma in Social Work—the professional qualification in the UK.*
DoH — *Department of Health.*
LGMB — *Local Government Management Board.*
NASW — *National Association of Social Workers (US)*
NVQ — *A system of National Vocational Awards and accreditation.*
NISW — *National Institute for Social Work.*
NISWIS — *The National Institute's Information Service.*
p-value — *Stands for statistical significance, i.e. the extent to which we can be sure beyond a reasonable doubt (usuallly 95%) that a relationship was not due to fluke or random error (see also χ^2).*
RAE — *Research Assessment Exercise.*
RCT — *Randomised Controlled Trial—a strict form of research comparing results from a randomised sample of those who receive services with those who do not, or who receive a lesser service.*
SPSS — *Statistical package for the social sciences.*
TOPSS — *Training Organisation for the Personal Social Services.*

Foreword

People who set up Centres for Evidence-based anything run the risk of being taunted with cries of 'And where's *your* evidence, then?' But Sheldon and his colleagues forestalled that possibility. The first thing their Centre for Evidence-based Social Services did was to organise a large-scale survey to provide a baseline for the work they were going to set in train: they wanted to know the current status of the evidence-based approach in their region, and what were the obstacles to be overcome.

This book reports the survey findings. It is a unique account. Some of what it tells us is quite depressing. However, it allows those who follow the fortunes of the Centre for Evidence-based Social Services to gauge where the enterprise started from and how far it has got. Better to know what one is up against, surely?

The Centre, a partnership between Exeter University and the Social Services Departments of the South West Region, and the Department of Health has achieved much in its short life: research, training, dissemination and—harder to specify but much to be admired—a sense of ownership among Directors and frontline workers alike. I have seen this with my own eyes.

More recent reports and newsletters from the Exeter Centre carry the story forward; but social services departments and universities everywhere can learn some salutary lessons from the results reported here. Short summaries have been circulated via CEBSS conferences, and this research has played a major role in shaping the CEBSS project, but there was always a need, now satisfied, for a fuller treatment so that the implications of this research (the largest survey of its type) might be debated nationally and internationally.

If these findings are not heeded and acted upon evidence-based practice will be difficult to develop and sustain in social care agencies, and that would be to the detriment of the people who need our help.

Barbara L. Hudson
Fellow of Green College
University of Oxford

Chapter 1

The Shock of the Old

The concern that effective help should be available to poor, troubled and otherwise needy people is as old as social work itself. Joseph Rowntree was much concerned with the issue, the American pioneer researcher Mary Richmond was writing about the impediments to the realisation of this aim on the eve of the Russian revolution (Richmond, 1917), and the first president of the National Association of Social Workers (NASW) made this the subject of his inaugural address in 1931. Here are his (worryingly modern-sounding) words:

> *I appeal to you, measure, evaluate, estimate, appraise your results in some form, in any terms that rest on anything beyond faith, assertion, and the 'illustrative case'. Let us do this for ourselves before some less knowledgeable and less gentle body takes us by the shoulders and pushes us into the street.*
>
> (Cabot, 1931: p6)

It is still possible to tease conference audiences with this quotation by reading it out and then attributing it to a contemporary source, either academic or governmental. 'Yes', the audiences nod concernedly, 'we really must embrace this new initiative.'

Yet the Social Work field, particularly in the United States, tried hard to put the matter of its usefulness beyond the reach of shifting political ideologies earlier than did any of the other helping professions. The first large-scale Randomised Controlled Trials (RCTs), which are the strictest tests of professional good intentions, were begun in the 1930s and reported in the 1940s and 1950s (Lehrman, 1949; Powers and Witmer, 1951; see Sheldon, 1986, for a review of this and later British work) whereas the first medical trials (of streptomycin for pulmonary tuberculosis: Daniels and Hill, 1952) brought an experimental approach into clinical medicine afterwards (just too late for George Orwell who died of TB thereabouts). The agriculturalists beat us all to this (Fisher, 1926).

The problem was that the results from the first social work experiments were almost wholly nil—nil draws, or worse, (Mullen and Dumpson, 1972; Fischer, 1973, 1976). Indeed these brave, early studies should have taught us long ago something that all the helping professions (including medicine) have only recently begun seriously to acknowledge, namely, that it is perfectly possible for good-hearted, well-meaning, reasonably clever, appropriately qualified, hard-working staff, employing the most promising contemporary approaches available to them, to make no difference at all to (or even on occasion to worsen) the condition of those whom they seek to assist. It still happens today (Gibbons et al., 1978; Byford et al., 1999; Wessely et al., 2000).

Clear negative findings do not, in a strict scientific sense, matter. Lost hopes aside, methodologically kosher but disappointing findings are very precious. They tell us, particularly in combination, what *not* to do and, potentially at least, provide arguments for the release of resources for more promising ventures. These large (and for the most part) well-conducted studies did eventually lead to a series of changes in practice favouring more focused and better-organised approaches which later stood up well under test, (Reid and Hanrahan, 1981; Sheldon, 1986; Macdonald and Sheldon, 1992; Macdonald, 1999). However, there are some more detailed points to be made:

1. The early negative findings came as a great surprise to everyone, both those closely involved in the research, and later readers of it. When consulted at various stages in the conduct of studies staff were almost always sanguine about the undoubted gains being made:

   One of the most fascinating pieces of information from this study involves the caseworkers. Throughout the programme, counsellors were asked on several occasions to list all the treatment group boys who they thought had 'substantially benefited' from the services offered by the project. Roughly two thirds of the boys were so listed. Further, at the end of the treatment over half of the boys volunteered that they had been helped by their caseworkers. Similarly, in a follow up of treatment group boys which included 254 boys where data could be found, global adjustment ratings suggested that two thirds were adjusting satisfactorily, a figure that could have easily been attributed to the effects of the project. However, when data on the control group were added to the picture, it changed dramatically, showing no difference between the boys on any indicators of delinquency or social functioning. It is not necessarily that the treatment boys were not doing well, it is more that their 'doing well' could not be attributed to the caseworkers' efforts, since control group boys were doing equally as well.

   (Powers and Witmer, 1951: p162)

2. The publication of scattered single studies with clear negative findings did little to alter professional attitudes, and where they were known about at all, they were seen as flukes. It was *reviews*, that is, collections of such material, that forced the conclusion upon us that just because particular approaches or patterns of service-provision are routine, congenial and familiar, they nevertheless tell us little at scientific level about their effectiveness (see Marshall et al., 2000, for a modern example of this from the case management

field). At a recent multi-disciplinary mental health conference the following quotation was read out, amended however, so that wherever the phrase 'case-management' occurred, the name of a mythical second-generation neuroleptic drug, Lususoproxine was substituted (lusus is Latin for joke):

Case management increased the numbers remaining in contact with services. Case management approximately doubled the numbers admitted to psychiatric hospital. Except for a positive finding on compliance from one study, case management showed no significant advantages over standard care on any psychiatric or social variable. Cost data did not favour case management but insufficient information was available to permit definitive conclusions.

(Marshall et al., 2000)

The audience was then asked what should happen in the light of this evidence, and overwhelmingly suggested that the medication should no longer be used. However, when they were let in on the little thought experiment, a substantial number, though sympathetic to the principle, thought that little could be done about social care interventions since they were embedded in national and local policies, and that different rules applied. Interestingly, the way forward in the field of relapse prevention and maintenance in the community for people with schizophrenia seems to be not abandonment of case-management, but the adoption of a more intensive, proactive, multi-disciplinary version of it called 'assertive outreach' (Marshall and Lockwood, 2000) which is achieving superior results, though with some cost implications.

However, getting back to our historical theme, the position in the early 1990s was that both reviews and single studies were showing increasingly positive results (78% of 94 screened outcome studies, see Macdonald and Sheldon, 1992) but that staff, inhabiting a workplace culture favouring action over reflection, and much pre-occupied with the new commercial principles which accompanied community care reforms (Griffiths, 1988) appeared rarely to have heard of these more promising findings (Sheldon, 1987a). However, as a result of the work of a few irritatingly persistent academics, the policy emphasis regarding social research gradually shifted towards problems regarding the dissemination of existing findings, for the commissioning of new research to be genuinely 'gap filling' (DoH, 1994), and for contractors to include in their applications for funding practical proposals for ensuring the potential future use of findings. In other words, though many hundreds of thousands of pounds of social care research had been commissioned, the question of who exactly might read the results, and what were the chances of their implementation, assumed increasing importance. Gore Vidal recently addressed this problem in a broader cultural context in the *New York Review of Books* when he observed that, 'At the present time, we probably have too many writers and not enough readers'.

Thus, under the influence of developments in the Health field, particularly those brought about by the Cochrane Collaboration (Cochrane, 1973; Maynard and Chalmers, 1997) new impetus was given to research and development schemes with research, practice, or service-development objectives as their *raison d'être*. Most notable of these, in our field, is the £2.5 million funding of the Centre for Evidence-Based Social Services (CEBSS) at the University of Exeter, a partnership project involving the DoH and 16 social service departments in the South and South West of England, and charged with the following aims:

1. To translate the results of existing research into service and practice development.
2. To ensure research findings are available to Social Services Departments when reviewing and changing service delivery, and are fed into the review process.
3. To collaborate with providers of DipSW and post-qualification courses to ensure that education and training in social work incorporates the knowledge available from research.
4. To improve the general dissemination of research findings to local policy makers, managers, practitioners, carers and service-users.
5. To commission new research where significant gaps in knowledge are identified.

With such promising contemporary developments in hand, why dwell on historical matters at all? There are three good reasons for such stubbornness:

1. One of the more sensible views of Karl Marx (paraphrasing Hegel in this instance) was that 'those who know no history are often condemned to relive it'. If there is any field in which this is true it is Social Work.
2. Our common experience in the social services is that new initiatives which ignore their historical roots, wither quickly when the limited supplies of political fertiliser dry up.
3. Large enterprises, when they seek to change behaviour rather than merely discourse, depend upon a widespread discussion of aims, purposes and results if they are to secure 'informed consent' from staff regarding the extra work to be done.

In other words, regarding this promising idea of evidence-based practice, enthusiasm should be tempered by remembering that the 'sieve of history' has large holes.

The Concept of Evidence-based Social Care

It is time now, having looked at the origins of the idea, to consider the implications of evidence-based practice in social services. Here is a short definition containing the principal aims (freely adapted from Sackett et al., 1996), advocates of the slightly chilling idea of evidence-based medicine since most of us thought it a settled matter shortly afer Dr Finlay arrived at Tannoch Brae:

Evidence-based social care is the conscientious, explicit and judicious use of current best evidence in making decisions regarding the welfare of those in need.

Conscientiousness

How do the key words in this quotation translate to the Social Work field?

Conscientious surely reminds us of our ethical obligations to clients, not least among which is to try to keep up to date on research which helps us understand the nature and development of personal and social problems, and to keep abreast of studies on the effectiveness of particular interventions which *might* ameliorate these. This is, after all, what we, as consumers, expect of those whose services we use, from medical and nursing staff to gas fitters. Surely social workers cannot be exempt from a similar obligation? Further, why should a single, apparently immunising dose of professional training be sufficient to equip us for these tasks? Are the problems that we face really so much less complex?

Hippocrates (400 BC) counselled his student physicians on the moral imperatives of intervention thus: 'First do your patient no harm'. Can it be said that social services staff do no harm? Just to mention the events on the Orkney Islands (Dalrymple, 1994), or at Cleveland (Butler Sloss, 1988) sadly puts this matter beyond doubt. Then there are sins of omission rather than of commission to consider, as in the many reports of the deaths of children in our care (Howitt, 1992; Sheldon, 1987b). The problem is that 'hard cases make bad laws'. Child death from abuse is statistically rare, but below this iceberg tip is a much larger mass of children suffering non-fatal, but serious physical and emotional injuries. True conscientiousness would imply much greater attention to these, whose cases do not make the Daily Mail leader page (Macdonald and Macdonald, 2000). Suicides and homicides by people with a psychiatric history are *statistically* rare (though it is worth noting that the former are much more likely than the latter), but below *this* iceberg tip is a mass of people with potentially spoilt lives who need our aid (Appleby, 1992, 1997). True conscientiousness would mean that a system would be constructed akin to that in aviation. There it is also rare crashes that make the headlines, although reports of much more frequent 'near misses' give the most valuable information against which to improve safety, provided that such events can be reported and analysed without draconian penalties ensuing, as they can in Aviation, but not in Social Work. The prospects for openness about mistakes and service-failures in Social Work are not good. One of the present authors has been urging the development of such a system on child-care conference audiences for fifteen years, receiving considerable encouragement for the idea that staff might report problems anonymously, but never receiving a single letter. Therefore this will not happen, unless a confidential structure is put in place, and the present system of learning nothing until it is too late, will continue.

Explicitness

Explicitness, that is, working in as open and contractual a way as possible with clients, has emerged as a key ingredient in effective helping over the last few decades (Reid and Shyne, 1968; Stein and Gambrill, 1977; Sheldon, 1980, 1986; Macdonald and Sheldon, 1992). It causes some problems though, and has done for some time as this early quotation (from two pioneer experimentalists) shows; it addresses the issue of what exactly is the distinctive contribution of social work and what constitutes good practice:

> These qualities cannot reside in the mind of someone in the agency who knows what they think is important but cannot express it because it is too subtle to be communicated or because it is a relationship so fragile that any attempt to measure it would destroy it.
>
> (Jones and Borgatta, 1972: p112)

The idea that basic scientific procedure is much too blunt an instrument with which to poke about in the necessarily mysterious dynamics of what passes between would-be helper and might-be helped was once the major obstacle to the goal of explicitness in our dealings with clients. Indeed, the idea is still in circulation. However, a new version of this problem has now arisen. Its origins lie in the community care reforms of the 1990s (a great, but politically compromised cause) wherein heart-warming phrases about 'needs led' services were later nullified by decisions that 'needs' for which there were no budgets, no facilities, or no conveniently available expertise, did not (in true Orwellian fashion) really count as needs. Transparency of decision-making and honesty about what existing funding can and cannot provide should surely be the aim in these matters. All the rest must be passed fearlessly to accountable politicians.

There are Idols which we call Idols of the Market.
For Men associate by Discourse, and a false and
Improper Imposition of Words strangely posesses
The Understanding, for Words absolutely force
The Understanding, and put all things into Confusion.

(Francis Bacon, *Norum Organnus Scientarum*, 1620: Section II, Aphorism VI)

Thus the enemies of explicitness are approaches such as 'methods-led', or, 'it feels right to me (I'm a natural)'; and 'this is what I've always done'. In other words, the answer's a group discussion, or a referral to a family centre, or care management—now what's the problem?

Organisational obstacles and the power of habit aside, the principle of explicitness demands a review of the available options with clients based upon a thorough assessment of their problems and needs and upon what is known from research on effective interventions in cases such as theirs. It requires also, clear and transparent goal-setting, and the building-in of progress-monitoring and evaluation procedures to every stage of our work (Sheldon, 1995, Chapter 5). The need for such precautions was never more eloquently expressed than in the following quotation:

> *The personal social services are large-scale experiments in helping those in need. It is both wasteful and irresponsible to set experiments in motion and to omit to record and analyse what happens. It makes no sense in terms of administrative efficiency, and however little intended, indicates a careless attitude towards human welfare.*

(Seebohm Report, 1968)

Judiciousness

The next key word in the working definition is *judicious*, that is, the exercise of sound, prudent, sensible, judgement. The stock of the Social Work field is not high in this regard. Considered pragmatism has been out of fashion for a decade and a half at least. We seem instead, lacking a healthy professional immune system, to be prone to infection by fads and fashions: some, on the face of it plausible, some less so (Sheldon and Macdonald, 1999). The case here is that not all that could be done should be done; and that not all things that staff like the idea of are sound; but that equally, some things that appear demanding or expensive in the short run turn out to be a bargain in the longer run. Potential risks arising from some, or no intervention, either in cases or in policies, should be thoroughly assessed and evaluated, but in the knowledge that not all eventualities can be predicted. All else is dangerous pretence (Parsloe, 2000). As was seen, the rise of 'full metal jacket' child protection squads from the 1980s onwards (under the influence of a short series of dramatic single cases) had the side-effect of thousands of families being brought automatically into a system virtually guaranteed to switch off future co-operation, and originally designed only for a few seriously dangerous situations. In the vast majority of cases (80 per cent of 20,000 cases, Thoburn et al., 1995) no further action was taken and few of the remaining 20 per cent got continued or substantial help. Only now is 're-focusing' on prevention beginning to make an impact on defensive practice of this kind, this after many nightmarish experiences being suffered by needy but not really wicked families.

In the Mental Health field we have moved, in a very few years, from large numbers of patients being detained unnecessarily in hospital, to large numbers of individuals struggling to cope in 'the community' (which doesn't always 'care'). Yet, contrary to the previous Minister of Health's view that 'the policy of community care has failed', beneficiaries largely take a more positive view (Macdonald and Sheldon, 1997; Leff, 1997). The media-inspired view that homicide rates have risen dramatically as a result of community care, is simply not borne out (Appleby, 1997) which should surely, given what else has been achieved, be a cause for modest celebration?

These then, are the challenges which confront the evidence-based social care movement in general, and the CEBSS project in particular, and so we turn next to questions regarding the changes in service-organisation and staff behaviour which would be required to achieve these aims, and then to our survey material, which gives a measure of the difficulties.

Organisational Implications of Evidence-based Approaches

If evidence-based social service provision were to become a reality (rather than just a laudable aspiration) then we would expect to see the following changes in the way the social work profession organises itself and social workers go about their work:

- There would be in place a well-qualified workforce within which knowledge and experience are regularly up-dated by training courses which make regular reference to research both on the nature and development of social problems and on what is known at an empirical level about the effectiveness of different approaches designed to address them.
- There would be qualifying courses which, as a matter of priority, would address and review the literature on the effectiveness of services and equip students critically to appraise the results reported therein.
- The profession would nurture a system of staff supervision which regularly draws upon research to inform decisions made about cases and projects, and wherein questions such as 'so, why are we proceeding in this way?', and 'on

what evidence?' would be seen as routine professional enquiries and not as a personal threat.

- Departmental meetings would regularly include references to research on what has been tried elsewhere, regionally, nationally and internationally, when services are being monitored or reviewed, or where departmental restructuring is in the offing, which it ubiquitously is, but often without benefit of supportive evidence for the changes envisaged and the value versus the costs involved.

- There would be a range of support facilities available to assist staff in their efforts to keep abreast of research relevant to their field, e.g. library facilities capable of delivering books and articles to enquirers, and able to distribute summaries of available evidence, with those in charge of them able to show that such services are regularly used.

- At an attitudinal level, there would be a workforce which takes some *personal* responsibility for acquainting itself with the empirical evidence on service-effectiveness, with a reasonably well-founded expectation of practical support from management for this necessary task.

- There would exist a range of collaborative arrangements between social services departments and local and regional universities and research institutes, so that each tangibly influences the work of the other, and within which each group of staff might unexceptionally be encountered on the corridors of the other pursuing common purposes.

Wishful thinking? Possibly, but without being starry eyed about it, the above template would obtrude in fewer places were it to be applied to Medicine, Health Care, or Clinical Psychology. Again, are the daunting problems that social workers face really *so* less complicated and *so* tractable? Do social work budgets, proportionally and comparatively, contain so little room for manoeuvre compared to the above groups, remembering that ignorance can also be very expensive?

These were the basic ideas, clusters of concern really, behind the framing of the CEBSS questionnaire (see Appendix 1). We sought through it to find out how far present arrangements match up to this ideal, and to discover what promising, reinforceable trends exist already, and what problems might require remedial attention.

Much is supposed about such issues, and much is assumed about the transferability of findings from the Health field. However, it is a plain fact that we have little directly-relevant empirical research on these matters. Thus the questionnaire was designed to gather new information on current attitudes and workplace conditions from as representative a group as possible from within the CEBSS consortium of sixteen departments. A unique opportunity, valuable in itself as a contribution to the literature, but also central to the planning and evaluation of the project itself.

Chapter 2

The Design and Content of the Questionnaire

The Sample

Fourteen departments (rising to sixteen with the inclusion of the new unitary authorities) participating in the CEBSS project were approached to supply information on the numbers, names and locations of front-line, professional-grade staff. This sample frame included social workers, senior social workers, team leaders, care or case managers, occupational therapists, and heads of residential facilities and their deputies. A further category was included to cope with 'hybrid' posts, viz: 'any member of staff with a key decision-making role, someone in an organising or front-line management post for whom it would be a reasonable expectation that research findings should play a role in influencing the way they go about their work'. This description produced a cluster of additional post-titles, e.g. foster care liaison officers, community project staff, and so forth.

Calculations as to the number of potential respondents needed to ensure a representative sample were made separately for each of the participating authorities. Four separate considerations informed this process (Monette et al., 1989; Oppenheim, 1992) viz:

1. The research questions: i.e. the number of variables being investigated in the study.
2. The level of population homogeneity: i.e. the degree of potential variability (regarding such factors as qualification level, function, gender, etc.) present within the population as a whole.
3. The precision level required (minimum 95 per cent confidence level).
4. The sampling fraction required to avoid under- or over-estimation of particular groups (see below).

The sample size was then increased by 30 per cent to compensate for the typically low response rate for postal questionnaires.

Due to the fact that sub-groups exist within this population, with different job descriptions and workplace conditions, we also took precautions to ensure proportional samples of field, residential and day care staff at this grade, plus occupational therapists.

The first finding to report from this preliminary stage in the exercise is that many departments experienced considerable difficulty in providing this basic information, either because of pressure of work, or, more commonly, because integrated data-bases containing names, workplace addresses and post-titles simply did not exist. There is simply no way of dodging the observation that large public-service departments, with extensive personnel sections, when questioned over a period of months as part of an agreed project, should really not have experienced such difficulty in identifying whom they employ, where, and for what purposes. We have been here before though; the Birch Committee (1972) on the employment of staff within social services virtually gave up on its *raison d'être* in the first chapter of its report for similar reasons of lack of reliable information. Nevertheless, not a satisfactory state of affairs in the age of computers. We did eventually solve these problems, but only by dogged persistence and through the supplementary use of payroll lists and internal telephone directories.

We next drew a proportionate, stratified random sample of 2285 professional-grade social services staff (this from an identified target population of 6994).

The Content of the Questionnaire

A 42-item instrument was designed (Appendix I) and was sent to staff in the region with a guarantee of confidentiality and a description of the purpose of the exercise. Interestingly, we received a number of individual and collective enquiries about the security of this approach before some staff were willing to co-operate. Such experiences call into question the extent to which the conditions of trust currently exist to support the aspiration of most departments to become 'learning organisations'.

The topics covered in the questionnaire were as follows:

Demographic information

This section covered the age, gender, and ethnicity of the respondents, as well as job-specific questions such as length of employment, post-title, type and level of qualifications, and the client-groups with which respondents mainly worked.

Departmental influences on the availability and use of research findings

Here we were concerned with questions regarding the extent to which research material was discussed during supervision sessions, departmental meetings, and on training courses. Participants were also asked whether facilities were available to assist them in keeping abreast of research findings, and how satisfied they were with those that were available. Next we sought to gather perceptions of the general level of support given by departments for such activities, and then views on how the day-to-day practical use of research could be further encouraged. Then came questions as to where respondents thought the main responsibility lay regarding responsibility for keeping abreast of research findings.

Existing reading habits and preferences

Reading habits were assessed in terms of the professionally-relevant publications seen by respondents, their opportunities for reading, and where any such reading took place. Respondents were then asked about their preferences for different types of reading material. We also enquired as to whether or why keeping up to date with professionally relevant publications might present difficulties.

Familiarity with research publications

In this section respondents were tested on their knowledge of two types of effectiveness research. They were asked to identify (against very liberal, sub-Paxman criteria) a client opinion study, and a randomised-controlled trial. Simple definitions of these methodologies were given on the page in order to minimise misinterpretation of the question.

Existing levels of knowledge of research issues and terms

Respondents' knowledge of research methods was also tested, in three ways:
1. Through awareness of factors that might produce positive responses in a client-opinion study other than those due to professional intervention.
2. Via a question regarding their confidence in appraising research findings.
3. Via a probe, i.e. a simple test contained in the questionnaire, "what did they understand by the term 'statistical significance?'"

Again, we were not expecting textbook definitions or explanations, just a basic grasp of the concept or issue.

Attitudes to evidence-based approaches

The perceived relevance of research in day-to-day practice and whether or how greater access might assist staff with their work were the main issues tackled in this section of the questionnaire.

Priorities for the Centre for Evidence-based Social Services Project

The objectives of the project were listed and participants were invited to rank the relevance of a range of activities that might help to further them.

Contacting Staff

A maximum of three mail-outs took place to each department, each with a covering letter encouraging staff to participate, guaranteeing confidentiality, and outlining the importance of the exercise as a 'diagnostic instrument' which would guide the work of the CEBSS partnership. Return rates climbed steadily at the second and third mail-out. All replies were sent directly to the University of Exeter.

Analysing the Responses

We received 1341 replies (58.7%) in total, which, because of the level of population homogeneity, can be regarded as representative of the stratum of the staff in the regional workforce that we wished to hear from. Demographic comparisons with the national workforce survey (LGMB/ADSS, 1997) suggest that demographic findings are, with a few exceptions (see below), in line with national figures.

Responses to closed questions were coded and entered into the statistical package SPSS 9.0. Replies to open-ended questions were converted into categorical data and then analysed quantitatively. Two researchers coded qualitative responses. Inter-reliability rates of 85 per cent were obtained, indicating a high level of consistency of interpretation. In cases where it was not appropriate to convert qualitative responses into categories because the degree of variability in the data did not allow it, emerging themes were identified by studying the first 100 responses and then continuing to analyse them until new clusters were no longer identifiable.

Frequencies were produced for all categorised variables and, where appropriate, cross-tabulations were made. In most cases, Pearson's chi-square test was employed; t-tests were used in the case of interval data.

For the purposes of this part of the analysis, respondents were classed as either social workers, occupational therapists, or 'other social care professionals'. This was determined by qualifications and job titles. Thus, social workers were those that gave this as their job title and had one of the following qualifications: Diploma in Social Work (DipSW), Certificate of Qualification in Social Work (CQSW), or Certificate in Social Services (CSS). Occupational therapists were those who gave this as their job title and held either a Diploma or a BSc in Occupational Therapy. 'Other social care professionals' were those who held a position that involved devising care programmes but who held other qualifications, e.g. NVQ awards.

On receipt of completed questionnaires we were forced to discard 115 responses since it was found that these individuals did not, in fact, fall into these categories. This decision was made after examining post titles and professional qualifications. Those excluded from the study were care assistants, occupational therapy assistants, and so forth. It is probable that these individuals had been given the questionnaire to fill in on behalf of those originally targeted in the study. Another problem was the variability of job titles across the different authorities, plus a tendency to give rather imposing titles to staff carrying out useful but essentially practical functions. Nevertheless, a total of 1226 respondents (53.7 per cent of the total number of targeted individuals) meeting the eligibility criteria were included in the study.

Chapter 3

Results from the Research

Demographic and Employment Data

The first section of the questionnaire sought to characterise respondents in terms of age, gender, ethnicity, qualifications, occupational titles and functions.

Our main findings in this regard are as follows:

- 67% of respondents described themselves as social workers; nearly 9% as occupational therapists, and 24% as 'other social care professionals'.
- 72% of respondents were female.
- The respondent's ages ranged from 21 to 64 years, producing an average age of 44 years (sd= 8.4).
- The length of employment in social services ranged from one to 33 years with an average of 13 years (sd=7.4). As the standard deviation for length of employment was high, the median was calculated and was found to be no different (median=12.0).
- Regarding ethnicity, 90.3% of respondents described themselves as either 'British', 'European', or 'Caucasian'. 1.5% of respondents described themselves as 'Asian' or 'Black'. 0.8% described themselves as 'other ethnic origin', e.g. Chinese, or mixed race (a further 7.3% did not give a response). Almost half of those describing themselves as Black or Asian were employed by Bristol or Gloucestershire Social Services. Clearly, this distribution reflects neither regional census data nor national workforce figures.

In respect of professional qualifications (Table 1), nearly a fifth of our sample (18.6%) held a Diploma in Social Work. A further 43.2% held a CQSW or CSS qualification (reflecting the age profile of the sample and the changing titles of qualifications). 8.7% held either a diploma or degree in occupational therapy. 16.2% of the sample was made up of staff who had qualifications in nursing or who held NVQs or other such qualifications, and the rest (14.7%) did not respond to this question. There were no great differences between these regional data for social workers and the LGMB/ADSS national figures (1997). Figures in tables and figures which follow are for total sample responses unless otherwise stated.

Table 1: Professional qualifications held by respondents	
Qualification	%
DipSW	18.6
CQSW/CSS	43.2
DipCOT	8.7
Other	16.2
Missing responses	13.4

63% of respondents reported having an academic qualification; 40.5% had a bachelor's degree, 10.9% a higher degree (predominantly at Masters level) and the rest held a scatter of diplomas and certificates. An association was found between professional origin and academic qualifications, with social workers significantly more likely to hold higher academic qualifications than occupational therapists (χ^2 = 28.7 df = 2, p<0.01). 61% of social workers held a Bachelors degree or above as opposed to 28% of occupational therapists.

We next enquired about membership of professional bodies. 71.6% of the respondents had no such membership. Occupational therapists were significantly more likely to be members of their professional organisation as compared to social workers and other social care professionals (χ^2 = 216.4, df = 1, p<0.001). Only 21.4% of social workers were so affiliated, but 87.6% of our sub-sample of occupational therapists were. This finding may indicate either ambivalence towards professional status and what it implies, it might be due to simple inertia, or it might be due to the current unattractiveness of the British Association of Social Workers (the professional body for social workers) and what it provides in way of incentives to membership. All that we can say is that these figures appear to be very low and show a rather weak sense of collective professional identity, or, to say the least, they depart from the usual and basic form of the expression of this.

Regarding the split between field and residential staff (Table 2), 68% of our respondents were field workers, with 20%, about equally, working in residential or day care settings. Occupational therapists and social workers (87.8%) were significantly more likely to work in a field setting than in residential or day care as compared with other social care professionals (38%) (χ^2 = 265.4, df= 1, p<0.001). The latter settings, despite much hand-wringing over the years, are where most staff with onerous responsibilities but with limited or no qualifications, work. All this is a source of continuing concern, given that it is in such facilities that many of our most needy clients tend to be placed. In other words, generally speaking, the greater the challenge, the less the training.

Table 2: Breakdown of type of work against professional status			
	Social worker (%)	Occupational therapist (%)	Othe social care professional (%)
Field	76.6	90.3	34.4
Residential or day care	11.9	3.5	55.5
Other	11.5	6.2	10.1
Total	100	100	100

Discussion of demographic and employment data

Despite the difficulties experienced in obtaining employment data required for this study, we seem to have achieved our main aim of collecting responses from a representative sample of professional-grade social care staff. As confirmed by national findings from the LGMB/ADSS survey (1997) the main characteristics of our sample closely resemble those of the national social services workforce across England. For example, 66.7% of the LGMB/ADSS sample were field workers. 71.9% were female. This compares with our figure of 72.7% for field workers, and 72% for female employees. There were also comparable percentages for level and type of professional qualifications. The exception was the higher proportion of occupational therapists in this study. The reason for this is that occupational therapists were specifically included to take part in this study and this was not the case for the LGMB/ADSS survey (see Table 3).

Table 3: Professional qualifications in the current study compared with national figures

Professional qualifications	Current study (%)	National (%)
Diploma in Social Work	26.1	26.3
CQSW	51.9	52.9
CSS	7.3	8.9
DipCOT/BSc in Occupational Therapy	14.7	1.8

Additional characteristics of the study's respondents were compared with the staff profile described in the Human Resources for Personal Social Services Report (LGMB/CCETSW, 1997). This reported that 80% of staff in their sample with a social work qualification are aged 35 years or over. The finding of the current study is that 86.7% of respondents fall into this age range. This age distribution somewhat contradicts media stereotypes of social workers, who are often depicted as young and lacking in life experience. In most cases staff are in mature middle age with a goodly period of years of professional experience behind them.

The LGMB also reported that 90% of occupational therapists in its sample were women and that their average age was 40 years. This is comparable with the current findings that 92.2% of the occupational therapists were women and their average was 43.0 years.

Why might such data, showing that social care is still predominantly a female occupation, surprise one? Perhaps because many of the senior managerial figures who appear in, or write for the media on social care issues are male?

Departmental Influences on the Use of Research

The questionnaire next investigated possible opportunities for, and obstacles to, the application of research findings to cases, and the level of consideration of such matters in supervision meetings, departmental meetings, or on departmental training courses.

Supervision

In our sample, staff supervision occurs for most (61.0%) on a monthly basis (Table 4). However, a sizeable minority of respondents have more frequent opportunities (23.7%), with 14.8% having to rely upon less frequent and ad-hoc arrangements.

Five respondents reported getting nothing at all. The vast majority perceived the quality of their supervision to be very or quite satisfactory (85.2%) a finding to celebrate given the pressures on staff time and the level of resources available to departments.

Table 4: Reported frequency of opportunities for supervision and consultation	
Frequency of supervision	%
Weekly or fortnightly	23.7
Monthly	61.0
Fewer than monthly opportunities	7.9
Ad-hoc opportunities only	6.9
No supervision at all	0.5

This shows that the tradition of staff supervision in social services, much admired in nearby fields is, if not thriving, then at least 'as well as can be expected' or better. Traditionally, the functions of supervision were seen to be:

1. To ensure accountability to the employing organisation for the extent and quality of work undertaken.
2. To offer an expert, second opinion on matters arising in cases.
3. To further the professional development of staff by directing their attention to the theoretical and research literature pertinent to their cases.
4. To offer personal support in cases where pressures and potential risks might lead to a loss of objectivity or a breakdown in working relationships with clients.

We were most concerned with Item 3. in the above list, and were interested to find out the extent to which supervision sessions included references to research findings.

It will be seen from Figure A below that, by report, only 5.0% of consultations contain regular discussion of research findings and their possible application. In 35.1% of cases this occasionally occurred (which is mildly encouraging), but if we consider the remaining 'hardly ever' and 'never' categories, we see that in 59.9% of consultations the issue is, worryingly, down the agenda. We say 'worryingly' because all that research is, is the screened and codified experience of others working with similar problems, and so one might have thought it

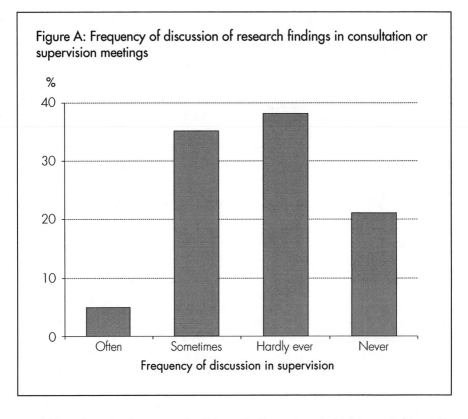

Figure A: Frequency of discussion of research findings in consultation or supervision meetings

would be, if not the first port of call in such discussions (which is probably *risk*), then at least the second, and certainly not something to be left out much of the time.

However, there is an interesting association in our data, in that those respondents who answered positively to a later question on the perceived relevance of research to their jobs are significantly more likely to be involved in such discussions with their supervisors (χ^2 = 14.98, df = 3.p<0.005). It appears therefore, that there is a two-way influence at work here, i.e. that some staff introduce these matters from personal interest or experience, and some supervisors and team leaders raise these matters in any case. These findings support evidence from the Health field (CRD, 1999) which suggests that exclusively 'top down' or 'bottom up' approaches to dissemination often neglect the fact that influences on workplace behaviour are probably reciprocal. In the CEBSS project we have taken account of this and increasingly bring groups of people from different strata of the same organisation together at our dissemination events. So far the results from this approach are encouraging (CEBSS, 1999; 2000).

Perhaps these matters of research and practice integration are raised more frequently in other departmental meetings where service effectiveness is being reviewed? We see some noteworthy increases in likelihood here, in that over 50% of the sample reported such discussions taking place often or sometimes. By no means do they appear to be a routine occurrence, but such issues are on the agenda some of the time, and therefore we have another potentially reinforceable trend.

Departmental meetings

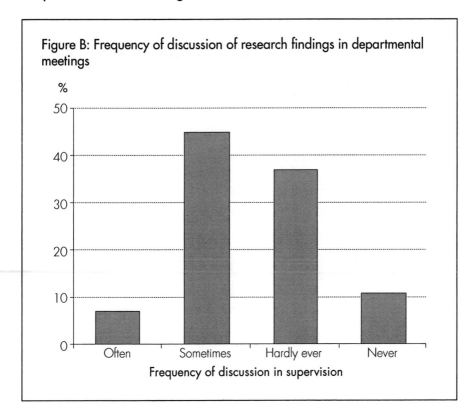

Figure B: Frequency of discussion of research findings in departmental meetings

Let us now turn to the question of whether research issues surface in other departmental meetings. It will be seen that Figure B. contains some encouraging data with 51.8% of respondents saying that this happens 'often' or 'sometimes'.

Nevertheless, the low 6.9% figure for 'often', and the 10.7% figure for 'never' reminds us (given that we were polling professional-grade staff) of how much there is to do before the incorporation of research findings into day-to-day decision-making becomes routine. The work of the CEBSS project (29 conferences for staff on the main research trends from effectiveness research; seminars for Councillors; over 40 specialist client-group conferences; training courses on accessing and interpreting research; meetings with senior managers, and so forth totalling 123 events to date) has been enthusiastically received (CEBSS, 1999, 2000) and so in the near future we should be in a position to see whether these problems have been influenced in the longer term. See Figure C for samples of findings.

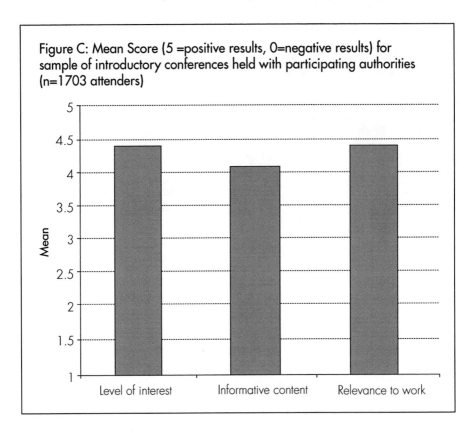

Figure C: Mean Score (5 =positive results, 0=negative results) for sample of introductory conferences held with participating authorities (n=1703 attenders)

Departmental training courses

The next possibility was that departmental training courses might make regular reference to research. Let us examine the issue. Expenditure in England and Wales on these post-qualification, departmental training courses currently stands at £22 million per year. Our figures (Fig. D) show that staff in our region attend, on average, four such courses per year (sd=3.06, median=4.0). Within social services, the majority of courses tend to be concerned with equipping staff with the knowledge to cope with new central government initiatives (e.g. 'Best Value'; 'Quality Protects') or to inform them of local policy changes. In terms of our data, there is a startling distribution for individual attendance. The shoulders of the curve are made up of 5.1% of staff who *never* attend such courses and on the other side, of decreasingly small numbers of 'training groupies' who attend between seven and 32 sessions per year, pointing to the possibility that personal interest strongly influences who gets access to what.

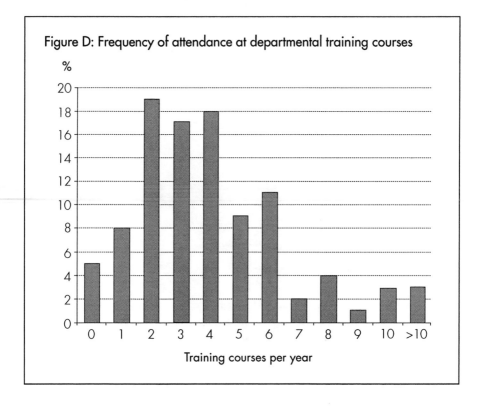

Figure D: Frequency of attendance at departmental training courses

Figure E1: Attendance at training courses on interpreting research findings

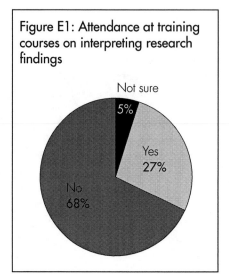

Figure E2: Attendance at training courses on using research findings at work

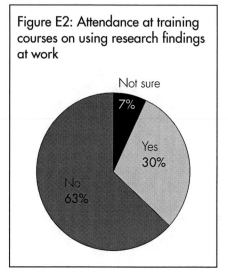

Figure F: Perceived departmental encouragement for respondents to keep abreast of research

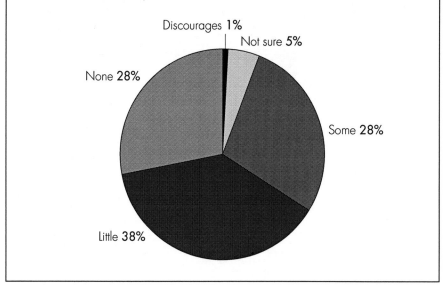

The question of frequency aside, what room is there on departmental courses for discussions of research findings? We see from Figure E that just under a third of the respondents have attended courses where such matters have been discussed. Again, we have a potentially reinforceable trend, even though take-up of opportunities for post-qualification training is more modest than in comparable professions, some of which require it rather than occasionally offer it.

Departmental encouragement

We next asked a general question to bring together the above issues, namely: 'To what extent do you feel that your department encourages you to keep abreast of the research literature relevant to your job'? Figure F (above) contains a summary of responses.

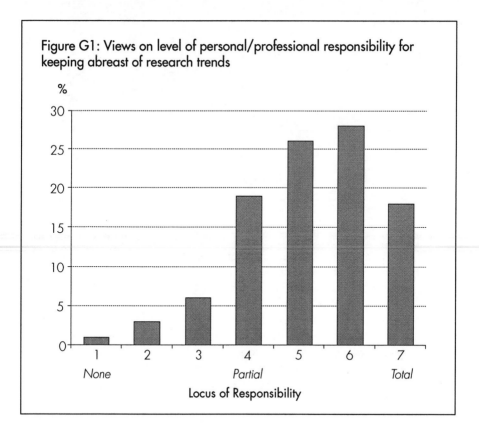

Figure G1: Views on level of personal/professional responsibility for keeping abreast of research trends

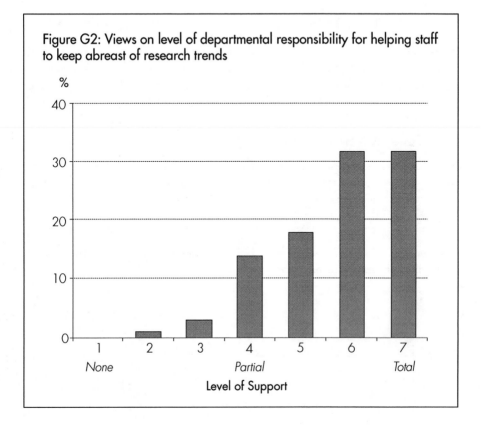

Figure G2: Views on level of departmental responsibility for helping staff to keep abreast of research trends

Leaving aside the plight of the one per cent of somewhat disaffected respondents who felt they were *discouraged* from attending to such matters(!) the meat in these data is the 66.3% of staff who thought that their employers provided 'little' or 'no' encouragement in the matter of using research to inform practice. There are, however, reinforceable trends in the above data in that 33.1% felt that they had 'a lot' or 'some' encouragement. Clearly we have a mountain to climb here. On the same point Celia Atherton, director of a sister organisation, the *Research in Practice* project at Dartington, observed at one of our 'Creating and Sustaining an evidence-based culture in social services conferences', 'so let's concentrate on the next 200 metres'—which is exactly the approach that CEBSS and its partners have been taking to such findings.

A question of responsibility

We next sought to find out about the extent to which staff thought that any responsibility to keep abreast of research pertinent to their jobs was primarily their own personal or professional obligation, or whether it was something for which employing organisations should largely be responsible.

Figures G1 and G2 show that most respondents, sensibly, assigned responsibility for the task both to themselves and to their employing organisation. However, there is a statistically significant tendency for both social workers (t=10.1; df=796; p<0.001) and other social care professionals (t=8.0; df=270; p<0.001) to see their departments as *more* responsible for encouraging this. Interestingly, this is not the case for occupational therapists as there is no significant difference between whether they assign primary responsibility to themselves or their department (t=0.9; df=113; ns).

That most respondents should see this matter as a joint responsibility is entirely what we hoped to see; the skew toward this function being seen by social workers as mainly a departmental responsibility probably may reflect a shift away from professional staff considering themselves to have a wider disciplinary affiliation beyond the terms of their contracts of employment. If government through policy and service frameworks, and managers through inspection and quality targets seek to control *everything*, then it may well be that a sense of a separate professional identity atrophies, as we have seen in education and health in the last twenty years.

However, there is another, contextual problem here. Social workers in particular, have long been unable to decide whether they really wish to belong to a profession, subscribing somewhat to the view of George Bernard Shaw that professions are 'a conspiracy against the laity'. So let us allow ourselves a parenthesis, and address the question of exactly what affiliation to a profession entails.

Here are the usual candidate rules:

Professional status or not?

- That there exists a distinctive body of knowledge to inform decision-making. We have such, without doubt, in the theoretical writing and the empirical studies, investigating both the nature of social and personal problems and studies of what might sensibly be done about them (Macdonald and Sheldon, 1992; Macdonald, 1999; Davies, 2000). The fact that this body of knowledge is augmented by contributions from other disciplines, e.g. psychology, sociology, health-care, is entirely in keeping with developments in other fields where the most exciting innovations have occurred because a few eccentric academics have hopped over disciplinary fences to see what is going on among the neighbours. Indeed, some distinguished authors (Wilson, 1998; Dennett, 1991) think that this is the way forward for modern scholarship, and that such attempts at 'consilience' (the integration of knowledge from different fields) is a sign of intellectual maturity, not of a lack of disciplinary identity.

- The next requirement is that staff who claim professional status should exercise influence over important matters, i.e. life and death, major life-chances and events. It was once held that only Law and Medicine fulfilled these categories. But do those in the social care services not also hold such matters in their hands? Failure in child protection has led regularly to the deaths of children (Howitt, 1992; Sheldon, 1987b); failure in mental health care sometimes leads to the deaths of clients or members of the public (Reed, 1997; Ritchie et al., 1994) or, much more frequently, to the suicides of clients themselves. The point is, that social care staff deal with a multitude of demanding, difficult, and sometimes dangerous problems. Staff need to be quite clever to sort these things out. It follows therefore, that they need to be well-informed about research findings reporting on the efforts of others who have tried various solutions and have either succeeded, succeeded a little, or failed. In other words, 'you're never alone with a research review', providing it is a good one.

- The next requirement is that there should be an ethical code in place. We have one, not perfect, but good enough (BASW, 1975 plus revisions). Moreover, all departments have their own quite exacting policies regarding the conduct of employees. Where we may perhaps fall short is that such pledges give only limited mention to the requirement to make use of best-available evidence as an ethical obligation. Foot dragging in this regard is a mistake, since there is, after all, little point in a published commitment to provide speedy and equal access to ineffective services.

Social Work clearly meets all the above criteria, and so our advice is to drop the single inverted commas which normally accompany the word *professional* in social services publications, since they indicate, a queasy uncertainty, which leaves us open to undue influence by others with less practical knowledge but more forceful opinions about how we should go about our work.

In case the reader is thinking that something has been left out of this list, namely, self-governance, then this matter can be quickly disposed of. No professions (not Law, not Medicine) are more than a little self-policing these days: the world has moved on, and, providing that politicians can resist obsessive-compulsiveness in these matters, appropriately so.

However, if we were to stop dithering about our professional standing, then some sharp responsibilities would also come our way regarding the need to demonstrate the cost-effectiveness of what we do, and our willingness to discriminate in favour of good-quality evidence as opposed to just 'doing what comes naturally' or what is par for the course in employing organisations. But then all this requires that staff have access to facilities that will enable them to obtain relevant, empirical studies in the first place. How do we fare here?

Availability of and satisfaction with library facilities

As figures H1 and H2 show, departmental library facilities in the region (as elsewhere outside it) leave much to be desired. Over one third of respondents report *no* opportunity for access, with a little under a tenth unsure whether their departments have a collection or not. Just under half of respondents who have such facilities find them unsatisfactory (44.7%). When we have discussed these figures at dissemination conferences, the common complaint is that library stocks contain, largely, internal policy documents and government publications; few modern books, and few journals.

This said, and lest we focus only on problems (an occupational hazard, perhaps), 55.3% of respondents reported that they both had access to, and were 'very' or 'quite' satisfied with existing arrangements (see Figures H1 amd H2). Thus there are examples of good practice available. The problem is that such positive developments are located in very few authorities. The best example in the CEBSS consortium is Hampshire (88.8% of their respondents registering satisfaction), which has a well-used, specialist library, with electronic search facilities and a delivery-to-desk facility, a model that has, through the CEBSS project, excited considerable interest elsewhere in the region. Other examples of good enough practice, as judged by respondents' satisfaction rates, come from Dorset, Somerset, Wiltshire and Cornwall as can be seen from Table 5 on p33.

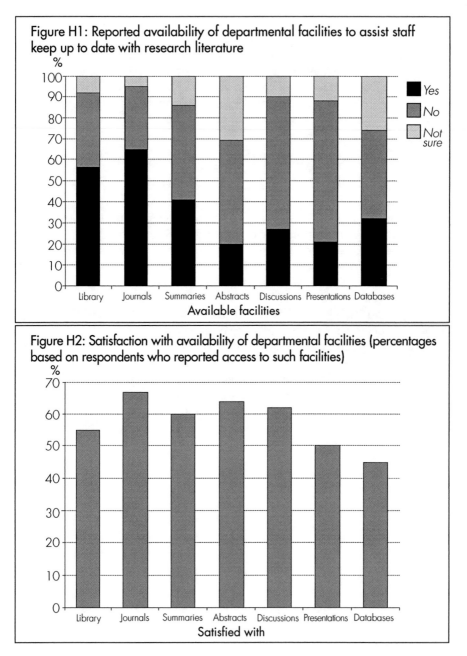

Figure H1: Reported availability of departmental facilities to assist staff keep up to date with research literature

Figure H2: Satisfaction with availability of departmental facilities (percentages based on respondents who reported access to such facilities)

Table 5: Highest rates of satisfaction with three facilities within the department

Facility	Highest rate of satisfaction (%)	2nd highest rate of satisfaction (%)	3rd highest rate of satisfaction (%)
Circulated journals	Dorset	Hampshire	Somerset
Library	Hampshire	Wiltshire	Cornwall
Research summaries	Hampshire	Wiltshire	Somerset

The joint CEBSS and National Institute for Social Work (NISW) Initiative (CEBSS, 1999) has made a start in alleviating the problems faced by staff regarding access to research publications and reviews. The main aim of this scheme is to ensure that getting hold of such material is a less time-consuming and frustrating business than hitherto. Through our collaboration with NISW we are firstly providing funded access to *Caredata*, an electronic social care database with UK and international coverage, for all the participating authorities in the CEBSS region. Access has been organised not only for social services departments but also for colleges and universities who offer qualifications in social care. *Caredata* can now be accessed free of charge within the CEBSS area on the Internet using passwords which are distributed via designated contact persons in each authority and educational institution.

Social services staff and managers can also request literature searches from the NISW Information Service (NISWIS), which they typically complete within three working days. Photocopies of articles found in *Caredata* can also be obtained through NISWIS, and CEBSS have encouraged the use of this service by distributing vouchers for use by the 16 participating authorities.

Finally, the initiative provides training by information officers and librarians specialising in social care. Our programme *Moving Forward with Research Online* introduces the CEBSS/NISW Initiative and includes workshops on using *Caredata* and other electronic databases, on searching the internet for social care research, and on how to make best use of library services. University of Exeter librarians join us at our 'Evaluation Clinics' where staff with an evaluation project in hand come to discuss methodological issues with CEBSS staff, and conduct searches on their behalf (CEBSS, 1999). Hence progress is being made to ensure that library and information services reach departments in the CEBSS project regardless of the access normally available.

Types of available facilities

Respondents were next invited to comment on any reasons for satisfaction or dissatisfaction with the facilities available to assist them in keeping abreast of research findings. The main practical problem seems to be that even if a library is technically available, travel to it is too time-consuming for regular use. The implication here is that those in charge of library services need to be proactive, to circulate summaries of research publications, particularly reviews of evidence, and to find ways to get such material quickly onto the desks and screens of staff, which was a major reason for satisfaction with the Hampshire service. A new generation of library and information officers already do this in related fields, especially Health, and have, from their own literature, a good grasp of exactly what is needed (Lopatin, 1997). The problem is that, in our field, more than modest investment in such services is the exception rather than the rule. The progress of evidence-based social services will stall at this point unless ways can be found to make access easier.

On line information

Electronic dissemination (already identified as a priority for the CEBSS project), is potentially the most effective means of overcoming this problem, but lack of ready access to computers, confounds any 'quick fix' solutions. However, there are encouraging developments in hand for an Electronic Library for Social Care, and the matter is at least on the political and professional agenda. One large, easily accessible, regularly up-dated electronic database with pre-appraised, good quality research material, is without doubt our best bet for the future, the alternative being a proliferation of isolated, local, short-life schemes, as is the case now.

In its early days, the CEBSS received a great many enquiries from frontline staff about particular fields, problems and cases. The appetite for knowledge and advice is thus certainly present. These 'helpline' enquiries, to which we responded whenever we could, threatened to swamp other work and are now being re-routed via library and training staff who can then call on us for further assistance if necessary. The present study and our day-to-day experience suggests that there are some sticky problems regarding access to good quality empirical studies, or even to good, theoretical writing, at present, but as illustrated in later findings, the appetite for something better is strong and persistent. Indeed, given rising interest in evidence-based services, the demand for better support services is likely to grow rapidly. But then, libraries are not just places or collections of books. The good ones will regularly monitor usage and have policies in place regarding the optimum range, quality of acquisitions and how to attract readers.

Circulated journals

Next we turn to another set of possibilities, namely, the circulation of journals, research summaries and abstracts which might help bridge the gap. The latter are important in providing accessible summaries of current evidence, e.g. the ubiquitous Joseph Rowntree *Findings* series and the excellent Barnardo's *What Works* series. Figure H1 shows that research summaries are getting through to practitioners to some degree (41.0%) though a large proportion do not have regular access (45.2%). The most promising figure is for circulated journals (65.1% having access, though 33.4% of such respondents consider them an unsatisfactory source of information).

Looking further into these surprisingly optimistic figures, and confessing here to a little professional naïveté, we see later from Table 6, that staff make little or no distinction between academic or practice journals containing empirical research content, e.g. *British Journal of Social Work*, *Child Abuse and Neglect*, *Journal of Mental Health*, and *Community Care* magazine. Very few respondents in fact, see anything other than *Community Care*, a worthwhile magazine and on the up, and now with a 'Research Matters' supplement which could, if it abandoned its *pot pourri* approach, develop into something very influential. Nevertheless, not a research journal in the accepted sense, and, understandably, containing only limited information on empirical findings. Thus, social care staff largely do not read what academics write for them. Nor is there much evidence that what academics write for each other, or for the Research Assessment Exercise (RAE), 'cascades' down to front line staff— the usual hope and justification for such work.

However, given that limited reading habits are a fact of life, there is an opportunity to be seized here. For if researchers could condense and make lively and readable (there's the rub) summaries of research and its implications, then they have here a large potential audience right on their doorsteps. The problem is that the RAE, on which university staff depend for their league table positions, would probably punish such foolhardiness.

Discussion groups and research presentations

On now to other possible sources of support, not based primarily on paper summaries of findings. What chances do staff have to take part in discussion groups or attend research presentations to hear about research trends and their implications? Figure H1 above shows such opportunities to be very limited. The implication here is that social services departments are probably not capitalising enough on the expertise they have in local universities (with whom, remember, they are supposed to be 'working in partnership' over the provision of training) nor perhaps on the talent available in their own research departments and that in nearby authorities. To have one department or section, whether academic or within social services, pumping out research findings, but to give so limited a priority to what happens afterwards, is self-defeating. This need not be so.

Some years ago, Royal Holloway College, University of London, instituted a series of early evening sessions entitled 'Research in Practice' for local social services staff (Sheldon, 1987b). These events involved lecturers giving summaries of what they considered to be the most relevant research on given topics (therefore requiring little preparation time) and then debating implications with local staff. Arguably, given the positive evaluations of this initiative, this *is* a 'quick fix' method that might be tried elsewhere, as indeed it has been, and very successfully, thanks to the indomitable Barbara Hudson, in the University of Oxford. Other institutions please copy. Social Services departments have some leverage here, since they provide placements largely through a 'gift relationship' with universities.

Obstacles to accessing facilities

Thus, having facilities notionally available is only half the answer, and it appears that the problem of access divides into a number of related issues:

- Time pressures make the carving out of study time, even if very case-specific, difficult.
- The limited size of collections and their content. Most libraries are quite small; their catalogued content (where this happens at all) is quite restricted in range and so there is often little to tempt new readers.
- In rural areas, the travelling distances can be daunting e.g. Salisbury to Trowbridge, Saltash to Truro.
- Then there is the problem of how best to publicise what is available. Interestingly, our survey shows a noteworthy minority of staff who *think* they have a library service and can even give an evaluation of its quality, except that, as a matter of fact, they do not. Then there are others in the sample who think they 'do not have' such a service, or are 'not sure', who, in fact, do. The obvious conclusion from all this is that library and information personnel need to have a higher profile; that they need to reach out to staff more, and that they need to campaign to increase the attractiveness of the services they provide. There has been plenty of support for such initiatives from the CEBSS project regional Directors. In short, the appetite is there; there is no lack of interest, rather a lack of facilities, a lack of money, and perhaps a lack of marketing flair.

● The next question on this issue is, who is in charge? Many departments with library and information services in name, give this responsibility to staff in training sections or elsewhere who already have enough to do. This has the effect of marginalising the service, and it is clear that we must move to a position where someone is employed specifically to run such facilities and to make them work. There are encouraging signs within the CEBSS project that this is beginning to happen (CEBSS Annual Report, 1999).

How could matters be improved?

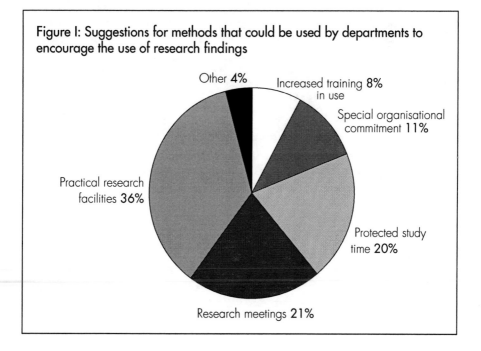

Figure I: Suggestions for methods that could be used by departments to encourage the use of research findings

Other 4%
Increased training 8% in use
Special organisational commitment 11%
Practical research facilities 36%
Protected study time 20%
Research meetings 21%

We next invited respondents to give their opinions on how the present rather disappointing situation could be improved (see Figure I). The main recommendation, accounting for a fifth of the suggestions on this issue, was for departments to organise protected study time. This is allowed for in some contracts of employment, and is *sometimes* backed by management. Happily, this is a concession being offered increasingly in CEBSS project departments and if such allowances can be extended will have a considerable symbolic as well as practical value in that management will be seen explicitly to be backing the idea that staff need to stock up on research information from time to time in order to do their jobs competently. An important consideration here will be to take the risk of not bureaucratising this process, because if staff have to register a reading plan, prove that they have carried it out, and then account for their work later in a report, it might be seen as not worth the effort. Probably we should invest in this idea, and deal with the question of how staff have used their time via standard staff appraisal systems. In other words, we should keep it simple.

Other important suggestions include the need for more research meetings and facilities enabling staff to keep up-to-date with research, views shared by CEBSS as discussed earlier. Management backing for the use of research within the workplace and the creation of a learning environment with a positive attitude towards evidence-based decision making were also mentioned by respondents.

Opportunities for Reading Professionally Relevant Publications

Having established the reading preferences of staff, we next tried to produce an estimate of the current extent of reading. We have to rely on self reports, and these are likely to be influenced by two potentially distorting influences:

- The general tendency (of all of us, probably) to overestimate the amount of time we spend reading, since it is a 'Good Thing'.
- The temptation for staff to answer pessimistically *pour encourager les autres* (Voltaire observed in 1759 that 'In England it is thought well to kill an Admiral from time to time to encourage others.').

Probably, our best check on these influences is to ask staff what they have learned from whatever reading they have been able to undertake, and the question regarding reading habits was 'When were you last able to read (rather than glance at) any literature pertinent to your job?'

The data are mildly encouraging as can be seen in Figure J, in that nearly half the sample (47.8%) claimed to have read something relevant within the last two weeks, which is a reasonable time scale for busy professional staff. Nevertheless a sizeable minority of the sample (34.0%) had not done so for between two weeks and a month. Then there is the problem that about a fifth (18.2%) of respondents had not read anything relevant to their work for at least the last six months, with 66 respondents within this group reporting 'too long to remember', a small, but worrying sub-group. Who are these people? Demographically, i.e. by gender, professional and academic qualifications held, they were not detectably different from the rest of the sample.

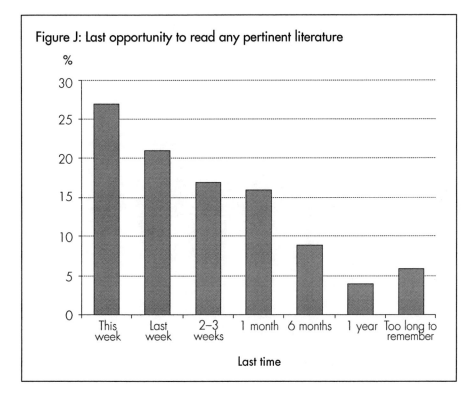

Figure J: Last opportunity to read any pertinent literature

The data (Figure K) reveal that staff, are most likely to read either a relevant magazine (87.8%) or internal policy documents (88.9%) or both. Nothing wrong with that, except that it is a somewhat restricted diet, unlikely to sustain the aims of evidence-based practice. There is a statistical association between frequency of when respondents last reported reading literature relevant to their work, and the likelihood of their reading research reviews and summaries (χ^2 = 11.9, df = 1, p<0.01) and academic journals (χ^2 = 15.1, df = 1, p<0.001). Respondents who were most likely to read either type of publication had read relevant literature within the last month as opposed to over six months ago. There was also a significant association between membership of a professional organisation and the likelihood of reading an academic journal (χ^2 = 7.2, df = 1, p<0.01). 45.2% of members were more likely to read such publications as opposed to 35.6% of non-members. However, membership did not significantly relate to the likelihood of reading research reviews (χ^2 = 2.0, df = 1, ns), probably the best, most reliable, and convenient way to keep abreast of findings.

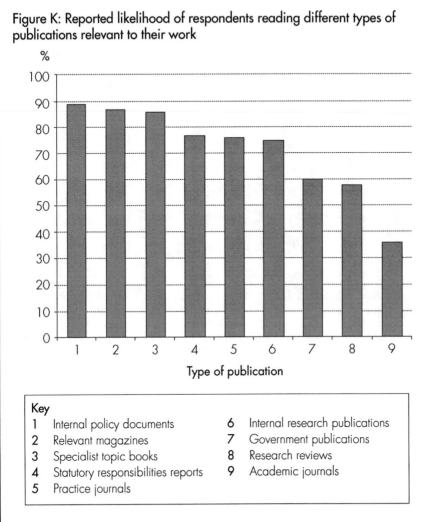

Figure K: Reported likelihood of respondents reading different types of publications relevant to their work

Key
1   Internal policy documents
2   Relevant magazines
3   Specialist topic books
4   Statutory responsibilities reports
5   Practice journals
6   Internal research publications
7   Government publications
8   Research reviews
9   Academic journals

Table 6: Types of relevant publications regularly accessed or subscribed to by respondents

Type of publication	Examples	%
Research or academic	Children and Society	5.2
	British Journal of Social Work	
Professional publication	Practice	2.1
Relevant magazine	Community Care	54.8
Charity or organisation	British Deaf News	3.4
newsletter or bulletin		
General references	Mind periodicals	0.7
Other combinations including	Law for Social Workers	1.8
at least one academic/research	British Journal of Occupational Therapy	14.2
or professional publication	Children UK	5.1
Other combinations	Community Care, The Psychologist,	12.8
	BHF, Macmillan (Cancer Relief)	

Almost three-quarters of the respondents had regular access to, or in a minority of cases, subscribed to, publications relevant to their work. In terms of professional groups, this breaks down to 87.8% of the occupational therapists, 75.6% of the social workers and 54.1% of the 'other social care professionals' stating that they have such access. Respondents who subscribed or had regular access were more likely to have read a pertinent article recently as compared to those who had no such access (χ^2 = 81.2, df = 6, p<0.001). This may seem like an obvious point, but as we know from the Health field potential access is one thing, and reading and use, quite another (Maynard and Chalmers, 1997): at least the potential is there.

The majority of these respondents identified that they had access to the magazine *Community Care* (65.1%) and within this group, 84.9% were social workers, 2.5% were occupational therapists and 12.6% were other social care professionals. Of those who had specified the publication to which they have access (n=768), professional publications and relevant magazines were predominantly accessed by social workers (81.3% and 82.2% respectively). 19.4% of our sample mentioned research or academic publications, but this group was mostly made up of occupational therapists (55.0%), *The British Journal of Occupational Therapy* and *Therapy Weekly* being the main publications mentioned (Table 6). There was a statistically significant association between respondents being members of a professional organisation and having regular access to research or academic publications ($\chi^2 = 128.7$, df=1, p<0.001). 43.4% of the respondents who belonged to such an association reported having regular access to relevant publications as opposed to 8.2% of those who did not belong to a professional organisation. Thus, either membership reflects professional attitudes which make reading more likely, or, as in the case of Occupational Therapists, it ensures that something relevant drops on the mat as part of the membership service.

This concentration on reading habits might look a little eccentric to some. We would wish to respond by saying that, whatever the opportunities potentially available, whatever the level of departmental support, whatever the frequency and depth of discussion in supervision or on training courses, evidence-based practice ultimately depends upon readers. And whether they read books, journal articles, research summaries, or material on computer screens, sufficient knowledge is required critically to appraise these texts and address the question of whether bias-reduction procedures are in place or not (CASP report, 1999; Macdonald and Sheldon, 1998a; Sheldon, in press).

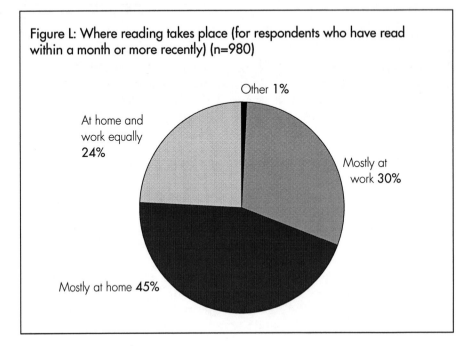

Figure L: Where reading takes place (for respondents who have read within a month or more recently) (n=980)

Other 1%

At home and work equally 24%

Mostly at work 30%

Mostly at home 45%

It will be seen from Figure L that *some* reading does take place at work, but that it is more likely to occur elsewhere for respondents who had read within a month or more recently. It is entirely in line with professional obligations that some reading and looking up should take place at work, so long as it does not interfere with other duties. Leaving aside the question of *what* is being accessed (though we have a good idea of this from previous questions; see Table 6) these figures contradict the stereotype that social services departments are places where *no* on-the-job reading is possible.

Next we looked at the obstacles to professionally relevant reading as perceived by staff. The favourite, 'Pressure of Work' was always likely to romp home in these stakes, but we needed empirical confirmation nonetheless. We presented potential respondents with six choices and Figure M shows our findings.

Figure M is rich in information on the circumstances which militate against the goal of evidence-based approaches to social service provision. The figures that stand out are that 98.3% of the sample (the largest cluster in the figure) who cite time-pressure at work as an important factor.

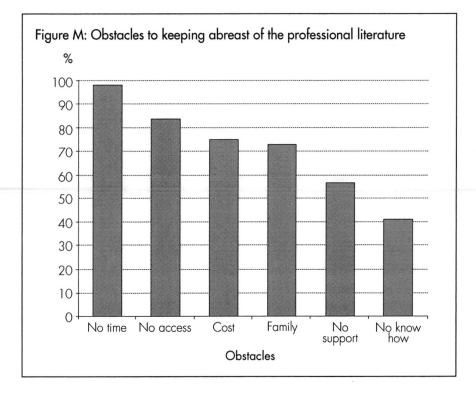

Figure M: Obstacles to keeping abreast of the professional literature

Discussions of these data with staff at conferences throughout the region suggest two things. Firstly, that this general reaction breaks down according to main areas of responsibility. Typically, child care staff have moderate-sized caseloads of very demanding clients and are preoccupied with risk (Parsloe, 2000). Secondly, as in Health and Education, and in local government generally, departmental accountability requirements are high, preoccupying, and rising. In our field it is apparent that the level of face-to-face contact with clients is going down in such circumstances. In the community care field, the obstacles most mentioned were sheer size of caseload and the logistics of servicing a wide range of more predictable needs but with severely restricted resources. Those working in the statutory Mental Health field (ASWs) are an exception to this simple split in opinions, and appear to be increasingly preoccupied with (not always evidentially-based) risks allegedly posed to the community by mentally ill people (Appleby, 1997).

The issue of access to literature is seen as a significant obstacle by 83.6% of respondents, justifying the priority being given within the project to the development of library and information services and the CEBSS/NISW initiative. The cost of journals and books ties in with the problem of availability. Institutional subscriptions, the sharing of subscription costs across the region, networking access to scattered sources of information according to a plan, is one possibility. That is, the development of a departmental 'inter-library loans' scheme. Electronic access will probably solve this problem over time. In the meantime, budgets are very stretched for this important activity.

The item on whether staff felt limited in their reading due to lack of knowledge of what to read and how to interpret it, produced a divided response. 40.8% saw this as an important obstacle. The CASP workshops funded by CEBSS is aimed at just this group, who have *some* access, but aren't sure *what* to access and how to interpret it. This is a major deficit in professional education, *indeed*, and is quite scandalous in our view.

Knowledge of Research Findings and Critical Appraisal Skills

We were in some trepidation about asking the next series of questions. Most questionnaires simply seek opinions on specific topics, but we thought it important to go beyond perceived confidence and familiarity and to test the actual knowledge of respondents on the key issues of research familiarity, understanding and appraisal. Therefore, our questionnaire moves from reported familiarity to three tests of actual knowledge.

Knowledge of evaluative research in general

Table 7: Reported knowledge of evaluative research in general; client opinion studies, and randomised controlled studies

	Evaluative (%)	Client opinion (%)	RCT (%)
Have read such material	43	35.7	5.0
Have not read such material	39.6	45.3	83.2
Not sure	17.4	18.9	11.9

We first asked participants about their familiarity with evaluative research using the question 'Have you read any evaluative research (studies testing out the effectiveness of an approach or service) relevant to your field?'. We have also pointedly asked such questions (verbally) at our evidence-based social care conferences, which have involved over 1700 staff, and the results are similar. Even the prospective data in Table 7 are disturbing, since all but a small minority of these respondents have been through university or professional education, an issue taken up later in this report. Nevertheless, we have over 40% of respondents *claiming* acquaintance. In order to test reported knowledge of evaluative research against actual knowledge, we asked those who answered in the affirmative to name a study which had been influential. Figure N indicates that plausible answers to specific enquiries are not the natural corollary of affirmative responses regarding general familiarity (your worships). Further, over 600 respondants did not register for the event at all.

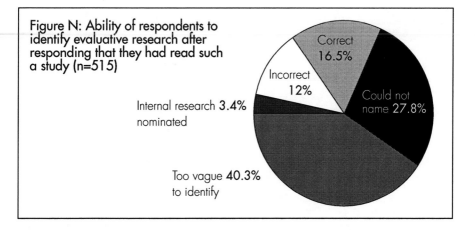

Figure N: Ability of respondents to identify evaluative research after responding that they had read such a study (n=515)

Correct 16.5%

Incorrect 12%

Could not name 27.8%

Internal research 3.4% nominated

Too vague 40.3% to identify

Knowledge of a client opinion study

We next asked a more specific question as to whether respondents had come across a published client-opinion study (that is, one which asks the consumers of services what they think of their effectiveness). This is the commonest form of social care research undertaken in Britain and so we hoped for an appreciable level of knowledge. Before we start analysing the above figures, we need to say something about our inclusion and exclusion rules. We checked each of the individual responses against our own (fairly extensive) knowledge of client opinion studies. Titles or authors with which we are not familiar were checked against databases such as *Caredata* to determine whether they were client opinion studies or not. In a few cases, where there was a sufficiently good description suggesting that the response was valid, it was included. Responses were independently checked by two members of CEBSS staff.

Client opinion studies are very important in that they gather considered responses, usually via in-depth interviews, from service-users and carers on their perceptions of the quality of services available to them and the effects which these produce. There is a substantial literature on which to draw (Rees, 1978; Fisher, 1983; Fisher et al., 1984; Macdonald and Sheldon, 1998) and this methodological approach is well in line with social services departments' aspirations to consult those on the receiving end of services and to adapt accordingly. Thus, some of this material should be reasonably well known one would have thought, but clearly this is not the case. 35.7% reported having come across a published client opinion study and a further 18.9% were not sure whether they had or not. Thus we have a situation where, the majority of a professional-grade sample of social care workers appear to lack any knowledge of these important findings and their implications for the improvement of services. This is simply not tenable for an allegedly educated workforce. But it gets worse.

Of the 432 who *said* they knew of a client opinion study (a mere 14.5% of the total sample), only 12.7% of respondents could, in fact, identify one against the very liberal inclusion criteria described above; 5.1% had a go, but were incorrect; 49.1% could not provide a title, author, or description (Figure O). There is a further point of concern in that of those who did make an accurate nomination, 41.8% identified *The Client Speaks* (Mayer and Timms, 1970), a pioneering piece of research, historically interesting, but somewhat flawed and relating to organisational conditions no longer to be found. Again it should be remembered that over 700 respondants did not even attempt this question.

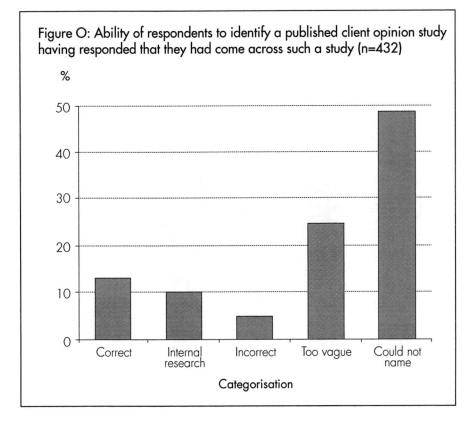

Figure O: Ability of respondents to identify a published client opinion study having responded that they had come across such a study (n=432)

Measures of critical appraisal skills

This next question was 'What findings might account for a positive result in a client-opinion study other than professional interaction?' We pre-prepared a list of candidate answers and to show a full understanding, respondents were expected to mention factors directly associated with clients changing circumstances during the course of the study, or the effects of participating in the study itself e.g. passage of time, maturational factors, simple attention, employment and income changes, or developments in family life. Broadly plausible factors, such as a new government policy, or media influences were included in the results.

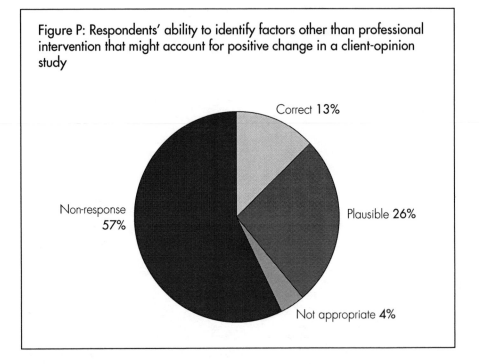

Figure P: Respondents' ability to identify factors other than professional intervention that might account for positive change in a client-opinion study

Correct 13%

Plausible 26%

Non-response 57%

Not appropriate 4%

It will be seen from Figure P above that only 13.5% of the total respondents could correctly answer the question. A further 25.9% gave plausible answers which showed *some* general familiarity with the issues but probably not a pointed understanding of most likely factors. 56.9% supplied no information. Examples of plausible responses are shown in Table 8.

As can be seen, the acceptance criteria were fairly broad. This is not rocket-science; we were not asking for the formula of a chi square test, rather for elementary logical thinking regarding the scope of a frequently used, largely qualitative, approach to service-evaluation research. These figures raise the basic question: are research methods courses no longer in place in professional training courses? If not, given their fundamental importance, why not, or if they are, what is going wrong with them?

This question was included to test whether the common, deceptively liberal-sounding view that all methodologies are somehow created equal, which has recently taken root on professional training courses (Adams et al., 1998) might not have the side-effect of persuading staff that questions of logic and basic science are not really their concern (Sheldon and Macdonald, 1999). The level of ignorance here is startling,

Table 8: Examples of responses given when respondents are asked to identify factors other than professional intervention that might account for a positive change in participants of a client opinion study

Response category	Example of quotes
Plausible answers	'Increased client empowerment' (respondent 931) 'Positive media publicity' (respondent 762)
Correct response	'The fact that clients are being asked and listened to' (respondent 352) 'Improvement in external stressors' (respondent 14) 'Better health' (respondent 462) 'New job or new relationship' (respondent 534)

and these, as with many other findings from this part of our research lead straight back to the content of professional training curricula (Macdonald and Sheldon, 1998). Remember that these are not questions about how to conduct research, only about how, given its methodology, to assign a degree of plausibility to findings, before applying its messages to some of the most needy and vulnerable members of society.

Further analyses conducted on the group who gave a fully correct or a plausible answer, showed that there were no significant associations between respondents' level of academic qualification and reported understanding of factors that might account for a positive change reported in a client opinion study (χ^2 = 5.3, df = 2, ns). Similarly, occupational function or job title was not significantly related (χ^2 = 5.5, df = 2, ns). Also, there was no significant association between respondents attending internal training courses on interpreting research findings and this variable (χ^2 = 0.571, df = 2, ns) which indicates that training from departments is unlikely to be the source of any knowledge of effectiveness research, and how it should be interpreted

As a corrective the following section looks at the various types of studies, their methodologies, procedures and levels of attributive confidence which should be known about by staff.

Systematic review of randomised-controlled trials, or meta-analysis of controlled trials
These look at comparisons of one approach with another standard or routine intervention across many studies of the same type. The procedure involves pre-

publication of a search strategy (usually involving both electronic databases and the hand-searching of journals) against specific inclusion and exclusion criteria. These cover issues regarding relevance and methodological sufficiency. Exhaustive searches of databases, an unvarnished presentation of results and implications, and regular up-dating are other hallmarks.

These studies maximise bias-reduction, so much so that almost always the effect size (degree of comparative benefit) against hard outcome indicators is reduced in comparison with other methodologies. If well-conducted they provide our most secure results. If producing negative outcomes, then they are still very valuable in advising what *not* to do.

Single experiments

These compare the effects of an intervention with an attention, placebo control, or other-treated condition, since attention and belief in the expertise of helpers also have strong effects. Best of all, (but rare) are studies with three conditions compared:

1. no intervention
2. standard intervention
3. test intervention

Random allocation to two service groups is required (within which procedures good-sized samples iron out differences between recipients). One group then receives an as consistent as possible exposure to the intervention under test. The other receives non-specific attention or another service. Outcomes are assessed against specific quantitative outcome indicators (e.g. re-admission to hospital, recidivism). Such findings can be backed up by qualitative data.

Such approaches provide for maximal bias reduction, but note that single studies can sometimes be errant (either positively or negatively). Standardising (that is making as uniform as possible) the intervention 'ingredients' poses problems, but large samples help to average out intervention differences. Sub-analysis of service-provider variations can also help to reduce this problem. Differential drop-out rates require particular attention.

Single experiments with a non-intervention control group

Random allocation of subjects is also a key factor here; some subjects get an as consistent as possible exposure to a given approach and others are left to their own devices.

Such studies have very substantial bias-reduction properties, but they do not tell us how far any differences between groups are due to specific approaches under test or non-specific attention factors. Replications or even concordant findings from quasi-experimental or pre-post studies increase plausibility.

Narrative reviews

These are not usually as exhaustive as systematic reviews and tend to have wider inclusion and exclusion criteria. They can also contain research using different methodologies. In such cases findings should be 'layered' i.e. it should be possible to see what results come in what proportion from which methodologies.

Authors draw up a list of topics which they wish to search (e.g., 'social work in general hospitals'; 'supported housing for learning disabled people') and then track down likely sources and look for emergent trends and implications.

Theses studies suffer from the problem of 'convenience samples' (i.e., sources readily available to the authors) and from a higher possibility of selective perception than where a very tight, pre-published protocol is in place. Nevertheless, very worthwhile and convenient summaries, sometimes coming close to later, more systematic reviews in their conclusions for less cost and labour. A good starting point for something more rigorous.

Quasi-experimental studies

These are comparison studies but without random allocation, therefore we can never be sure that we are comparing like with like, though case-matching helps moderately to increase confidence.

An under-used investigative method since it compares the results (usually pre and post) between areas where an approach is in use with a comparable area where it is not. Very useful in social services, where different interventions are routinely introduced in one area and not in another.

Pre/post tests

Sometimes known as time-series designs, these procedures compare problems and gains on a before and after basis in a single sample.

Baseline, i.e. pre-intervention (preferably standardised) measures are taken in key problem areas prior to intervention, (see Fischer and Corcoran, 1994 for an accessible manual). They are then repeated at the end of the programme for comparison purposes.

Most evaluations in social services are post-only (see below) and so it is difficult to calculate the value-added. This approach takes 'snapshots' of functions on a before and after basis. Nevertheless it cannot determine the extent to which any improvements which occur are due to the mere passage of time (maturational factors) or to other collateral factors unconnected with the intervention.

Post test only measures

This approach reviews outcomes only, without benefit of specific pre-intervention (baseline) measures.

A sample is chosen against criteria of need, type and extent of problem(s). The intervention is made, and then measures of outcomes are taken.

Since most social services approaches and projects are still not evaluated at all, this is better than nothing. It can be improved by standardised referral criteria being in place at the outset.

This short list of methodological approaches is presented here as a model of what it might be reasonable for professionally grounded staff to know about when evaluating research that they might make use of.

Knowledge of experimental studies

We next sought to investigate respondents' knowledge of studies which partly for practical reasons, and partly because of methodological timidity, are sadly, always likely to be a minority element in our literature but which nevertheless provide us with our most secure results regarding which patterns of intervention should be copied or perhaps even abandoned. That is, we were concerned to know what our sample knew of randomised-controlled trials (RCTs) of different service patterns (Marshall et al, 2000; Stein and Gambrill, 1977; Cohen and Mannarino, 1996).

Only a tiny proportion of respondents felt they could identify an RCT so respondents were much less sanguine than with the client-opinion study question. There are two elements to these data. Although 5.0% thought that they could identify an RCT, in fact less than 1% of respondents managed it when the next question was asked. The question was: if *yes*, can you recall the title of such a study or its authors? This leaves an astounding 99% of respondents who could not correctly identify an RCT study. Again, a very worrying finding given (a) that this is a professional-grade sample; (b) that a clear description of what was being asked for was given in the questionnaire, so there could be few if any grounds for confusion. Again, a convincing stab at the question with a recognisable description would have been accepted.

Knowledge of basic statistics

The interesting thing about RCTs is that if other promising results from client-opinion studies and pre-post comparisons are further tested using this approach, then the apparent therapeutic value of the intervention might well drop due to the bias-reduction properties of randomisation and the inclusion of a control group. This is also true in psychology, psychiatry, psychotherapy and just about everywhere else. But, nevertheless even modest gains tell us what to reinforce in our practice and in our policies. The point is, however, that given that we are dealing usually with comparatively modest increments of differences between those who get

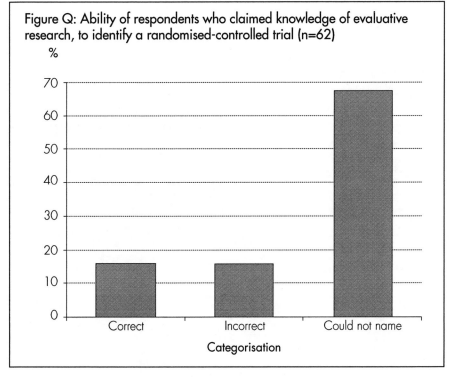

Figure Q: Ability of respondents who claimed knowledge of evaluative research, to identify a randomised-controlled trial (n=62)

something and those who get either nothing, or a standard service, detecting the degree of useful change in the sample becomes a matter of statistics. In other words we must apply statistical tests to measure the degree of comparative change against hard, that is, non-negotiable, indicators and calculate how far above chance levels they are. Thus the second critical appraisal question asked in the questionnaire sought to find out what knowledge respondents had of the term 'statistical significance'. The definition of this term for rating responses, used descriptions given in seven different books on research methods. (Greene and D'Oliveira, 1989; Whitaker and Archer, 1989; Herbert, 1990; Grinnell, 1981; Powers et al., 1985; Grady and Wallston, 1988; Mitchell and Jolley, 1988). From these texts, criteria representing three levels of understanding of the term were developed (Table 9).

The point here is that staff who read research articles need to know what is meant by 'statistical significance' and its place in drawing conclusions from the data. For example, it is necessary to understand this term when considering whether a reported difference between interventions or groups suggests a change should be made to current practice, or whether comparisons of effects are too small to justify this.

Table 9: Respondent's understanding of 'statistical significance'

Level of understanding	Criteria	Examples
Limited or no understanding	Inaccurate answer	'Something can be said to be statistically significant if it reaches in repeatable studies a certain large percentage recurrence, usually 5% or 15%' (respondent 355). 'That the sample used was large enough to reflect a real trend' (respondent 805).
Partial understanding	Mention of the role of chance, but not specifically related	'The difference in outcome is accounted for by the factor(s) under research' (respondent 717). 'Something could be due to other factors, not always what was done' (respondent 116).
Full understanding	Results/findings, or a difference in the data, were unlikely to be attributable to chance	'An outcome is statistically significant if, according to some accepted level of probability, it is unlikely to be due to chance alone' (respondent 99) 'The greater the statistical significance the lesser the likelihood of chance' (respondent 346).

Knowledge of what is meant by the boring 'p-value', is pretty dismal across the authorities, as shown in this study. We approached the issue in two stages, first via a measure of perceived confidence, then a test of actual knowledge for those who reported some confidence.

Table 10: Reported knowledge of the term 'statistical significance' (n-1159)

Yes	37.6%
Not sure	32.9%
No	29.5%

As can be seen in Table 10, over a third of our sample stated prospectively that they understood the term, though in fact only 3.9% of that group (16 people) showed full understanding of it, with 12.6% appearing to have a partial understanding. A worrying 64% of those who said they knew what the term meant, gave an inappropriate answer (see Figure R). It is unlikely, therefore, that the majority of respondents were equipped via their professional or subsequent training critically to appraise a research study pertinent to their work, should they have come across one. That only 6.2% of a representative sample of professional grade staff could give even a roughly accurate definition of this term (we included respondents who came within striking distance) must surely be a cause for concern. Again, the implications for professional training are obvious. We should not be using our professional training time to turn out academic researchers, but *surely* we should be equipping staff with enough knowledge to evaluate the meaning of differences in comparison research and whether they are above the level of chance variations.

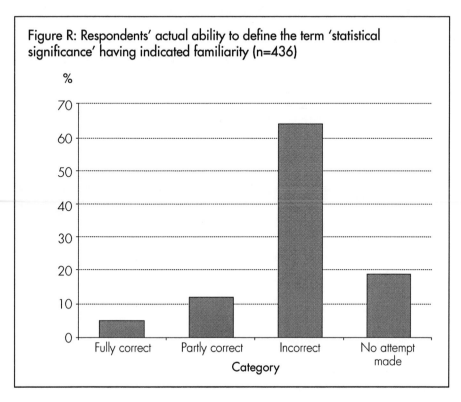

Figure R: Respondents' actual ability to define the term 'statistical significance' having indicated familiarity (n=436)

Please be assured that we were not looking for fine detail in these open-ended responses, only some knowledge of the idea that differences of outcome could be merely due to chance. This is very basic first year knowledge for most disciplines who make use of empirical comparisons, so why not for social workers? It is not, by the way, just a point about technical knowledge, it is an ethical matter. To bleat on about the latter, but not to address the former is, in practical terms, an unsustainable position. Neither a head over heart, nor a heart over head position will do in our field.

Critical appraisal of research materials

As can be seen from the foregoing, we asked two types of question in this study: perceived confidence, and actual knowledge. The gap between the two is often quite wide. As a further check on this, having asked the testing questions described above, we asked again about the self-perceived ability of staff critically to appraise a research article. Table 11 shows that nearly half the sample were sanguine about this question, though our critical appraisal training figures do not support this optimistic view.

Table 11: Perceived levels of confidence in critically appraising research articles relevant to social care

Perception of ability to critically appraise a research article	%
Very confident	6.4
Quite confident	43.0
Not very confident	39.3
Not at all confident	11.3

These findings show:

- A very low baseline of knowledge and skills: though the articles and the books on this issue have been available to professional training course staff for many years (Gibbs and Gambrill, 1996).
- That when given access to suitable training, staff respond well (CEBSS, 1999).

The policy implications for the new General Council and its attendant training organisation (TOPPS) are obvious, too.

With the results referred to above in mind, the CEBSS project commissioned an extensive programme of critical appraisal skills training for staff to teach the techniques necessary to separate wheat from chaff, and the levels of attributive confidence derivable from research studies (see above). These courses were well received, and our evaluations show not only very substantial over-subscription and high levels of satisfaction but also substantive gains in knowledge and skills (CASP Report 1999). A further round of training has therefore been started, this time including social care academics and practice teachers.

Perceived Relevance of Research to Professional Practice

This section of the questionnaire sought to gather the perceptions of staff on the general relevance of research to practice; the way in which such findings either do, or might influence the way they go about their jobs, what they gain or hope to gain from the use of research, and the ways in which practice might actually be influenced by greater knowledge of findings. Then we asked respondents to give an example of how a given study had influenced their work. Here are the data:

Table 12: Views on the relevance of research to the job	
Very	42.0%
Quite	47.9%
Not very	9.2%
Not at all	0.9%

At an attitudinal level these findings are most promising, with nearly 90% of respondents expressing the view that research is 'very' or 'quite' relevant to their work. Thus it is not the *idea* of a closer connection between research and practice that causes difficulties. This sample of staff clearly does not see itself as merely a collection of artisans or technicians who just need to know about the practicalities of a set of straightforward duties.

There was a statistically significant association between professional groupings and how relevant respondents saw research to be to their work (χ^2 = 37.8, df = 3, p<0.001). 46.1% of social workers and occupational therapists saw research as 'very relevant' to their jobs, as opposed to 28.9% of other social care professionals.

Taking the general sentiment that the application of research findings to practice is a 'good thing', we next asked a question on how far this is a practical reality.

How much does research affect practice?

Table 13: Extent to which research findings inform day-to-day practice	
All the time	7.4%
Quite often	46.4%
Rarely	42.1%
Not at all	4.1%

If we compare Table 13 above with Table 12 some interesting differences emerge:

- Although 42.0% of respondents in the previous table think research 'very relevant' to practice, only 7.4% in the above table reported frequent usage.
- Another telling contrast is between the over 90% who thought research was 'very' or 'quite' relevant to their practice and the 42.1% who 'rarely' made use of it.

Thus there is a sizeable gap in these data between beliefs and aspirations and their practical expression in the workplace; a continuing theme in this study, unfortunately.

Of respondents who reported that research findings informed their day-to-day practice 'all of the time', *all* stated that research was 'very' (75%) or 'quite' (25%) relevant to their jobs (see Table 14), so no dissonance there.

Participants who said that they received 'a lot' or 'some' encouragement from their departments reported that research findings more frequently informed their day-to-day practice (Table 15). There was a significant association between these two factors (χ^2 = 71.6, df = 3, p<0.001). There were also significant associations between whether respondents reported having access to library facilities (χ^2 = 20.8, df = 3, p<0.001), circulated journals (χ^2 = 12.8, df = 3, p<0.01), research summaries (χ^2 = 44.9, df = 3, p<0.001), abstracts services (χ^2 = 11.5, df = 3, p<0.01) or research presentations (χ^2 = 39.7, df = 3, p<0.001) and the frequency with which they said research findings informed their day-to-day practice (Figure S). However, there was no significant association between whether they subscribe to, or had regular access to, an academic or research publication (χ^2 = 1.0, df = 3, ns) and the latter variable, which again suggests that academic publications have less influence on practice, or at least on perceptions of what research material is used in practice, than most academics would like to think.

Next came a prospective question. The context here is that should it be possible (through the CEBSS project, and other national influences such as Research in

Table 14: Findings informing day-to-day practice versus relevance of research to job

	Very relevant	Quite relevant	Not very relevant	Not at all relevant
All the time	75.0%	25.0%	0%	0%
Quite often	52.1%	45.4%	2.5%	0%
Rarely	27.3%	55.1%	17.4%	0.2%
Not at all	20.8%	37.5%	20.8%	20.8%

Table 15: A comparison of perception of departmental encouragement to keep up-to-date against frequency of research findings informing day-to-day practice

Perception of departmental encouragement to keep up-to-date with research	Research findings informing day-to-day practice all of the time or quite often (%)
A lot of encouragement	70.7
Some encouragement	70.2
A little encouragement	50.5
No encouragement at all	39.5

Practice) to overcome some of the obstacles to the routine availability of research, and what influences on practice would be most looked for?

The key information in Figure T (below) is the 60.3% of respondents whose primary interest was in knowledge of effective helping techniques. This interest is well-confirmed within the CEBSS project by the level of enthusiasm for conferences and training events which review 'what works' in the context of given problems. We have completed over 120 of these in three years and even though we work with large audiences the events are always over-subscribed. This has implications, again for both qualifying and departmental training, our strong impression being that staff are not much acquainted with the literature on effectiveness (as opposed to broad policy and contextual factors).

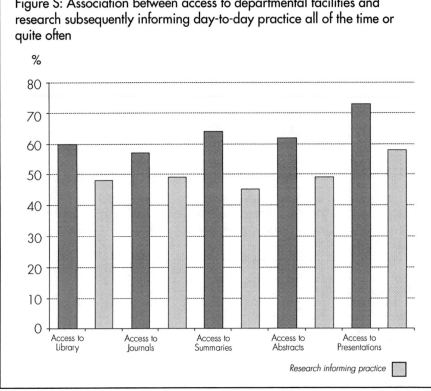

Figure S: Association between access to departmental facilities and research subsequently informing day-to-day practice all of the time or quite often

It appears therefore that what to do and say when working face to face with clients and what research-derived guidelines to follow, though seriously under-taught, are nevertheless the main pre-occupation of staff, after simple survival. It will also be seen that a fifth of respondents selected 'greater knowledge of the nature of social problems' to improve their assessments as the first priority. Many of the assessment schedules in widespread use in departments are rather atheoretical in this regard, in other words, they focus on very practical, physical concerns and ignore the psychological and social complexities of many of the needs and problems we have to address (Parsloe, 2000). Tellingly, effectiveness research shows that a close 'logical fit' between a research-derived understanding of the aetiology of problems, and what is then proposed as a means to ameliorate them, is the best predictor of positive outcomes (Macdonald and Sheldon, 1992; Sheldon and Macdonald, 1999) and 10% wisely doubled up their selection options accordingly (Figure T).

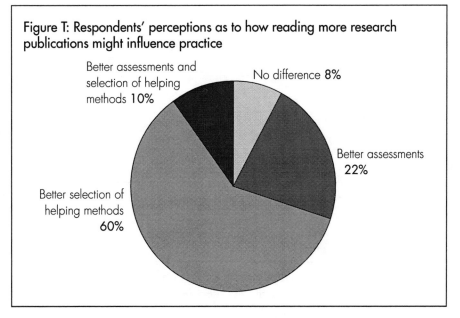

Figure T: Respondents' perceptions as to how reading more research publications might influence practice

Better assessments and selection of helping methods 10%

No difference 8%

Better assessments 22%

Better selection of helping methods 60%

Potential and actual improvements to practice

Having found out what appetites exist among staff, we turned next to improvements in practice which might or might not be expected to occur should access to research be improved.

It will be seen in Table 16 that respondents are either very sanguine or at least comfortably optimistic about this prospect. Given the pressure of work in departments and the many and increasing accountability demands on their time, these findings must be seen as a vote of confidence in the idea that greater knowledge from research of good quality would directly influence practice; useful interventions being, let us remind ourselves, what social care staff are for.

Table 16: Prospective level of improvement to practice given increased access to research literature

Definitely	32.4%
Maybe	64.5%
Already read enough	1.4%
Definitely not	1.7%

We next asked a more pointed question as to whether respondents could think of any way in which previous acquaintance with research findings had changed their practice (Table 17), and then, if yes, we asked them to indicate 'how'?

Table 17: Whether practice has been changed as a result of reading research material	
Yes	51.1%
No	27.2%
Not sure	21.6%

Table 18 (below) contains some typical responses:

Table 18: Ways in which practice has been changed as a result of reading research material
'Think more widely about issues. Also particular therapeutic techniques e.g. cognitive behavioural therapy and assessment skills. Also more able to contribute to decision-making in meetings' (respondent 647).
'Ray Wyre's work on sexual offending revolutionised my understanding of perpetrators' (respondent 15).
'Messages from Research' suggests that social services should not be so punitive in cases of child abuse, and in line with departmental policy I have tried to be more supportive. Moreover, other research I have read implies that we're not objective enough, so I am more careful to make sure that I have exact information on a referral and check out myself information I have been given by my clients, rather than just relying on their word' (respondent 415).
'Recently reading a report on the risks to life involved in transferring elderly people from one home to another, made me far more sensitive to the problems when I was involved in re-settling people from a care home which was recently de-registered' (respondent 27).
'R.A. Parker's studies of fostering breakdown produced a prediction table. Used in practice the prediction table assisted in matching foster homes to specific children and indicated the likely problem areas, and therefore the focus of intervention. This enables the worker to be more assertive in foster home selection and to use working time more productively on issues that matter' (respondent 304).

These, and other responses show that there are some intelligent readers out there, looking for support for an idea they accept. Of the half of our sample who contributed a qualitative comment, the majority gave short, but nonetheless general statements, e.g.: 'used as a point of reference' (respondent 14) which tells us little about substantive connections between reading and subsequent action. Also, the problem of respondents making little or no distinction between a magazine article, theoretical book or a research study, is present: exactly the same confusion that Brown and McCulloch found twenty five years ago (Brown and McCulloch, 1975). Thus, research and practice integration is visible, but in small pockets as yet.

Expectations of the Centre for Evidence-based Social Services

This section of the questionnaire sought the advice of staff on where the CEBSS project should concentrate its efforts. We provided an extensive menu of possible priorities derived in part from existing studies of the effectiveness of dissemination strategies (predominantly from Health), from the implications of the aims of the project set out by the Department of Health, and from experience over many years of trying to produce a closer union between research, practice, and service-development. In short, a fishing expedition. Table 19 is a complex but themed array of possibilities which we used in the early stages of the project to guide our activities. The responses fall into six specific areas:

- consultancy and advice-giving
- improving access to research
- dissemination of research information
- training on research topics
- working with specific professional groups
- promoting the use of research in general

We did not wish to constrain repondents in their choices, but rather, via a scale ranging from 'very important' to 'definitely not', to establish the priorities of the staff with whom we sought to collaborate.

Over three-quarters of the respondents indicated that all areas were important (probably true, but impractical). Nine out of ten reported that advising local policy makers and training departments on current research trends, publishing research reviews, and training in specific approaches which have a good research track record were important. Worryingly though, given the level of critical appraisal skill demonstrated, measures to address this problem received the lowest priory rating.

The next question enquired into any misgivings that staff might have about the idea of evidence-based social services, definitions of what is entailed having

Table 19: Percentage of respondents rating as important activities in which the Centre for Evidence-based Social Services could be involved

Area	Specific activity	Priority ratings (%)
Training on topics	Training in research methodology and how to interpret studies	59.5
Improve access to research	Setting up electronic databases of findings	67.7
Disseminate research information	Holding periodic conferences on research trends	68.4
Training trainers	Training local dissemination personnel	72.4
Promotion of local research	Filling gaps in available research	73.6
Working with professional groups	Working with local librarians on information needs in social services	73.8
Training on topics	General training on the concept of evidence-based approaches	78.8
Promotion of local research	Encouraging local research and evaluation exercises	85.5
Improve access to research	Help to gain better access to research material	86.0
Working with frontline managers	Training team leaders and supervisors	87.4
Working with academics	Working with staff from Diploma in Social Work and other professional courses	87.8
Dialogue with service users and carers	Working with users and carers groups to develop research agenda	88.0
Working with selected professional groups	Training other supervisors and mentors	88.3
Consultancy and advice-giving	Advising senior management	88.7
Consultancy and advice-giving	Advising training departments on current research	90.6
Consultancy and advice-giving	Advising local policy makers on current research trends	90.9
Training on topics	Training in specific approaches which have a good research track record	91.6
Disseminate research information	Publishing research reviews and summaries with practice implications spelt out	92.3

been given at the front of the questionnaire and fairly explicitly present in the questions asked subsequently. There is a small literature on this issue and contributors at dissemination events sometimes raise the questions:

- Is this just another fad?
- Is there a covert management agenda behind the idea?
- Who decides what counts as evidence?

In order to see how widespread any misgivings might be outside the somewhat self-selected sample of conference and training event attendees, we first produced a scale, and then invited comments. Here are some typical views (n = 1018).

Misgivings and doubts expressed regarding the use of research findings in the workplace

Possible use of research without due critical appraisal

- 'Research needs to have been properly undertaken and reported. People need to be able to understand it.' (respondent 52)
- 'As long as the stats aren't lies. As long as the inputs are good and the outcomes can be demonstrated.' (respondent 172)
- 'Believe research needs to be understood and used analytically and critically...range of studies needs to be appraised etc. to not be at risk of interpretation and application.' (respondent 368)

Misuse or abuse of research findings

- 'I was worried about research findings being used to excuse cuts within services.' (respondent 146)
- '...is very trendy at present but can easily be misapplied and justify bad practice.' (respondent 714)
- 'Danger of the anthropological 'bongo-bongo' mentality creeping in—one can always produce something to justify a point of view and give it credibility or respectability.' (respondent 131)

Concerns regarding the relevance of research to own practice

- 'It entirely depends on whether the research is relevant to the client group and carers involved.' (respondent 66)
- 'Research would have to be relevant to service delivery in a particular area with a particular client group.' (respondent 760)
- 'I am unsure about doing 'fashionable things' and flavour of the month solutions.' (respondent 140)

- 'Quality v. quantity comes to mind but sometimes research findings seem far removed from actual possibilities in practice.' (respondent 8)
- 'At what stage do the research findings become accepted as sufficiently 'sound' to be used in service delivery and planning.' (respondent 724)

Constraints on resources for putting research into practice

- 'In a service which is short in funds and is asked for cuts every year, my misgivings would be that an already overworked staff group would have even higher (and more unrealistic) demands placed upon it without the corresponding increase in time and resources.' (respondent 504)
- 'I think working practice based on evidence is an appropriate way to work but I think for social services at operational level, it will be a difficult concept to introduce as people are overloaded, have experienced too much change and feel de-skilled as it is.' (respondent 740)
- 'Does this mean even more paper work: both reading and writing?' (respondent 189)
- 'Will require additional time during assessment and care management of each case: is this available or possible in current climate?' (respondent 154)

Lack of departmental commitment to the evidence-based approach

- 'We have seen new innovations based on research implemented then over turned.' (respondent 8)
- 'The department appears to be employing multiple approaches and this is often reinforced by poorly supported, often untrained personnel. Demands on resources are such that intervention occurs at critical point often, despite knowledge that early intervention may result in better outcome.' (respondent 684)
- 'Any changes resulting directly from research tend to take a long time to reach the front-line or probably I would be retired before they were effective.' (respondent 365)
- 'Family group conferences cost money therefore not implemented although research evidence is there.' (respondent 432)

Research findings need to be disseminated in a user-friendly manner

- 'I have concerns that research may be too academic or highbrow to be easily digested and interpreted into action plans.' (respondent 104)
- 'Research must be written up succinctly and clearly, with good summaries to encourage harassed workers to read it.' (respondent 418)
- 'Using evidence from research is fine but dissemination methods for all information need looking at.' (respondent 35)

Again, the results (Figure U below) are overwhelmingly positive with over half the sample having no misgivings, and a more cautious fifth having only 'some misgivings' which was a surprise to us coming as it does from a group of front-line staff over whom new initiatives flow, year in year out. A very encouraging response. The 'nothing new' and 'don't like the idea' responses accounted for only 5.5% of reactions. This appeared to us, therefore, as a vote of confidence in the idea of evidence-based practice and the aims of the CEBSS project. The open-ended section asked respondents to explain any doubts or misgivings about greater emphasis being placed on research evidence in planning and delivering social services. This produced themes relating to the use of research and the conducting of research. Misgivings and doubts regarding the use of research findings concentrated on organisational issues and the complexities of applying research to practice including the need for related skills. In terms of conducting research, the main themes were that the right people, with service users and carers as an essential part of the equation, are often not consulted, sufficient resources are not allocated to support such activities, and that research does not

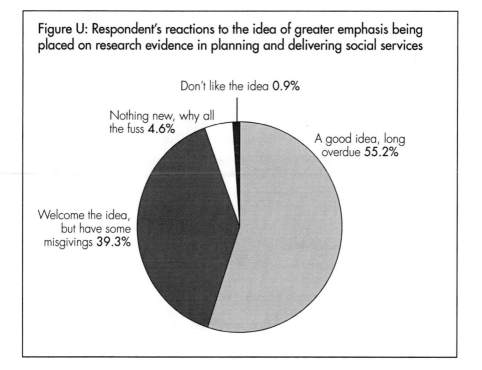

Figure U: Respondent's reactions to the idea of greater emphasis being placed on research evidence in planning and delivering social services

Don't like the idea **0.9%**

Nothing new, why all the fuss **4.6%**

A good idea, long overdue **55.2%**

Welcome the idea, but have some misgivings **39.3%**

keep up with the speed at which changes take place within departments. Hence it can be seen that misgivings on the whole are not due to a lack of support for the *idea* of greater emphasis being placed on research evidence in planning and delivering social services, but more about the complex nature of what is being suggested given current work pressures and established customs.

The next question also sought the advice of front-line staff. The CEBSS project has the capacity to:

- Fund primary research where gaps in the literature are identified.
- Lend its support, and some limited grant-aid to partnership research and development projects undertaken in local authorities (we have five such preventative projects underway at the time of writing).
- Provide training based on research findings where staff do not feel adequately equipped by training to deal with particular problems.

We asked respondents to select three priority areas which they thought were in most need of further research based on problems encountered in their workplace. The areas selected by respondents included questions as diverse as issues on assessment of children, to the organisation of care for older clients. There were three main themes in these qualitative data, plus a scatter of local preoccupations.

Potential for further research identified by respondents, based on problems encountered in their workplace

Understanding client problems

- 'What is 'normal' sexual behaviour for under 5s?' (Respondent 828)
- 'Input of parental break-up on children within families?' (Respondent 582)
- 'Assessments of out-of-control adolescents or adolescent mental health problems which are effective?' (Respondent 582)
- 'Research re under-65s, into how many would use suitable day care centres if they were available.' (Respondent 702)

Effectiveness of client services

- 'Treatment or therapeutic outcomes of perpetrators of abuse…Usefulness of CPR in terms of professional commitment to the process'. (Respondent 5)
- 'The most effective ways of working with young people whose criminality is directly linked with their drug use…How departmental policies and procedures actually contribute to the difficulties they are set up to ameliorate?' (Respondent 795)

- 'The most effective way of managing foster placements to ensure children don't remain longer than absolutely necessary in placement.' (Respondent 398)
- 'The impact of specialist training, e.g. family therapy and counselling on practice: is this useful or superfluous..? Effective interventions with families who despite years of social work support have not changed in a way which offers better life for the children.' (Respondent 368)

Organisation of Services
- 'Joint working with health: especially in the field of discharge from hospital.' (Respondent 220)

Research commissioned by CEBSS

We have 'gap-filling' projects on the stocks, viz:
- A trial of whether training foster carers in behaviour-management techniques reduces disruption to placement and improves quality of service for all concerned (University of Bristol).
- A study of a rehabilitation scheme for elderly people leaving acute care (Lomax et al., 1999), its staying power and cost effectiveness (University of Exeter/Devon Social Services).
- A study of the effectiveness of 'matching needs and services in child care' policies in one regional authority (University of Bristol).
- A comparative study of utility and the effects of a family conference approach versus standard child protection procedures (Wiltshire Social Services/ University of Bath/University of Portsmouth).

In addition, we offer, for example, methodological support to the Cornwall Social Services Child and Adolescent Mental Health Project (CAMHS), a comparative study of early intervention with children creating cause for concern at home and at school, and the Somerset Social Services project testing out the effectiveness of a co-ordinated approach between Social Services, Health Education and the Police.

Respondents views of CEBSS' chances of success

Having heard something about the aims of evidence-based practice in general and the CEBSS project in particular, respondents were next asked to give us an opinion on the chances of success of such an initiative (Figure V, below).

The perceived odds here are less favourable than early attitudinal responses relevant to the issue indicate. The balance of testimony favours an optimistic

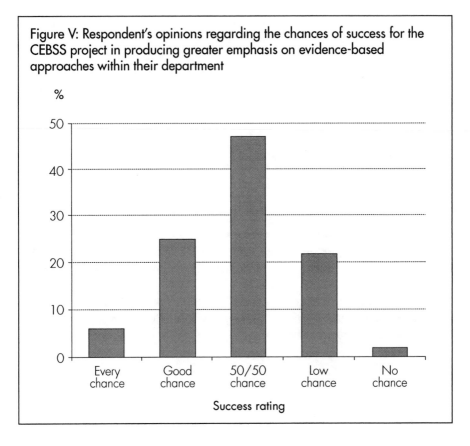

Figure V: Respondent's opinions regarding the chances of success for the CEBSS project in producing greater emphasis on evidence-based approaches within their department

view, with about a third of staff expressing confidence; but the 'evens' bet (always a safe option unless the consequences of losing are dire, which they may be in this case) constitutes the largest grouping of responses. Perceptions of risk vary with the potential outcome either way. Most of us would be gravely concerned about undergoing an operation with only a 50/50 chance of survival; most of us would be very anxious if told by a tutor that our chances of passing an exam were 50/50. However the apparent reasons behind these responses were interesting. Some comments mirror earlier findings and indicate that respondents have limited faith in CEBSS, and other fellow travelling organisations, being able to overcome the strong organisational barriers within Social Services.

Examples of respondents' views on the chance of success within the CEBSS project

- '50% chance of failure because pressure of work in child care social work means (1) no opportunity in the working week to become proactively involved and (2) low staff morale.' (respondent 621)
- 'The department was reorganised on 1st October so staff are reacting to the changes. Once things have settled back on an even keel, there should be a good chance of success.' (respondent 16)
- 'I feel that colleagues could be genuinely interested in an evidence-based approach if they, and myself, had the time to both learn more about the concept and read and use research.' (respondent 216)
- '...a staff divide has developed between management and the workforce. This has caused a lack of trust to any external influence.' (respondent 309)
- 'I am not sure about the commitment of senior management staff to this approach given their focus on budgets and management strategies.' (respondent 483)
- 'The department is far too busy to consider this issue and when it occurs it is dismissed due to lack of funds. There is no training or very little going on for social workers in care management: most of the training is for managers and untrained staff that are now expected to do the bulk of the work.' (respondent 59)
- 'We have no money at all. End of story.' (respondent 449)

Obstacles to Evidence-based Services

We were next concerned to elicit from respondents information on what they saw as the obstacles to evidence-based service provision. The 14 item menu (Figure W) covers workplace conditions, ideological opposition to the idea, resource constraints, and morale issues. Respondents were asked to make four choices in rank order. The top obstacle, pressure of work in the department, will come as no real surprise, though we needed to confirm the fact.

The next most important obstacle identified by respondents was funding. In practical terms this could mean the inability to find the money for free study time, additional training courses, Internet access, or the purchase of new publications for the departmental library. CEBSS now has initiatives in place to assist with all the above problems but these are necessarily limited in scope, and the comparative under funding of social services in proportionate comparison to Health remains as a serious obstacle to developments in our field.

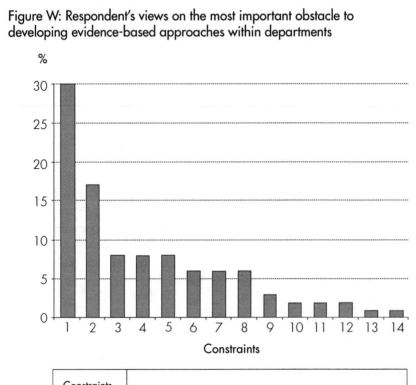

Figure W: Respondent's views on the most important obstacle to developing evidence-based approaches within departments

Constraints	
1	Pressure of work
2	Funding
3	Lack of knowledge about research
4	Lack of management support
5	Policies leave no room for innovation
6	Academic results are not the same as real practice
7	Low staff morale
8	Lack of back-up facilities
9	Inadequate training in interpreting research
10	Can't cope with any more change
11	It's a passing fad
12	Distrust of a narrow scientific approach
13	Social work owes more to art than science
14	There's a hidden agenda

A further six factors in the ranking were nominated by over 7% of respondents as the second, third or fourth most important obstacle. These are as follows:

- governmental and departmental policies leave little room for innovation
- lack of knowledge of research and how to interpret it
- academic results are one thing, realities of practice another
- lack of management support
- low staff morale
- lack of back-up facilities

Distrust of 'narrow scientific' approaches, social work 'owing more to art than science' and thinking that 'there is a hidden agenda' were three factors that were not seen as being important obstacles to developing evidence-based approaches within departments, which is something of a relief, though it would have once been a very surprising finding (see Brewer and Lait, 1980). These authors once tartly observed that 'if social work is an art, then let it be funded by the Arts Council': a view for which we retain a sneaking sympathy.

Chapter 4

Discussion

The purpose of this research project, as previously indicated was to:

- Help fill a gap in a sparse literature on a set of issues of increasing importance within the social services.
- Act as a 'diagnostic instrument' against which to plan and evaluate the various approaches to dissemination and training to be used in the CEBSS project.

The third section of the questionnaire regarding attitudes to the idea of evidence-based approaches sought a view from the field staff in the region on what our priorities should be. These latter responses are heart-warming stuff. The level of enthusiasm for the idea of evidence-based practice and service-development is palpable, as it always is at our dissemination events. The advice on where to place our bets, both from the scales and menus, and from the qualitative sections of the questionnaire is astute and thoughtful, though everywhere it warns us of the many routine disincentives to thoughtful consideration prior to intervention, and of the low (though rising) level of practical support for the idea of a continuously and strategically re-educated workforce. One of the present authors, having been involved in reviewing evidence on effective services for some years, is of the opinion that such a positive affirmation would not have been forthcoming a few years ago. Certainly, those staff who did receive training in effectiveness research and its implications in the past tended to find it interesting (Sheldon, 1987b) but these were, as it were, a largely self-selected sample. The present survey sample had received little more than a set of aims, but they rather liked the sound of them. They particularly liked the emphasis on effective *practice*, this after years of emphasis on structural change accompanied by not always well-informed debates about the *raison d'être* of the social services. Now, structural, managerial, 'top down' change *can* lead to better channels of communication; it *can* remove anomalies in the way staff are deployed. Indeed, we are just about to embark upon another phase of this as we are, at long last, being required to address the rather patchy, ad hoc working relationships which we have with Health (Care Standards Bill 2000). However, structural change can, also, at worst, be just a reflex adjustment away from whatever there was in favour of something new, usually on the basis of limited evidence, 'new board of directors, new manager, new strip, new game plan' as they say in football (or if they don't, they should).

The point is that we need to give attention to what is and is not happening in all the layers of our services (CEBSS, 2000). Over the past few years we have somewhat neglected the quality of face-to-face social work with clients, the very issues which staff in the present survey, and service-users, as revealed by client-opinion research and internal service-evaluations, are most concerned. The influences which persuaded us to attend to different priorities than these were largely political. A belief grew up in the 1980s that professional staff could not be counted upon for other than self-serving advice. A new managerial agenda was drawn up at the hands of politicians and senior figures from the commercial world on the assumption that public services, including Health, Social Care, and Education, would benefit greatly from an injection of competition, even if this had to be deliberately engineered. Then we saw the creation of what one of the present authors has referred to as 'the reinvention of the East German economy inside the public services of Britain (Sheldon, 1987). The process was begun by the implementation of the Griffiths Report in 1988. Sir Roy Griffiths was the financial head of the Sainsbury supermarket chain, and we must pause here, with a proper sense of humility not extended to us, to consider what a supermarket organised by social workers would be like? Even here there were *some* benefits; it is indeed an ill wind that blows nobody any good. Managerial control of services was much improved; strategic priorities were clarified so that the public began to see that within a given budget (a political matter) some things could be delivered, and other things not. 'Must do', 'nice to do', 'need not do (at least not by ourselves)' discussions became more transparent. However, this managerial model, saw social services departments as likely to be more cost-effective if they came to resemble B & Q hardware stores with a limited range of standardised 'products' more or less fit for most predictable needs. The problem in the social care field is that although, if we squint our eyes a little when we look, some needs *are* largely practical (e.g. support for frail elderly people at home), many are not. The sheer range of our functions is simply not apprehended by politicians. We deal with relapse in acute mental illness, fostering breakdown, child sexual abuse and its effects, juvenile crime, the needs of learning-disabled people in the community, the counselling of parents whose children have just died, and so on and so forth. Many of these awful problems require an individualised, and, research shows, an evidence-based, 'bespoke' set of services (Macdonald and Sheldon, 1992). 'Horses for courses' is an economical summary of effectiveness research trends: a 'logical fit' between needs and services.

Turning now to the more specific findings of this research, we propose to begin by addressing the more formidable and entrenched of the obstacles it reveals, other items having been dealt with in the text in any case. The list of aims for the CEBSS project are presented in rough priority order and we are charged with addressing all of them. However, on the basis of the evidence from our questionnaire, and from experiences at dissemination events, we propose that these priorities should be realigned. That is, that since we are dealing with a large sample of professional grade staff (not care assistants carrying out only routine practice duties), the low level of knowledge among them of empirical research on the nature of the problems they face daily, or of studies of the effectiveness of different approaches and service patterns (regarding which there are substantial literatures), suggest to us that there is something wrong with professional training. Influencing this problem was seen as a background matter in the initial stages of the CEBSS project, but since it keeps re-appearing as a cause of the present state of affairs, it deserves more considered attention.

Implications of Findings for Professional Training

Professional education and training, whatever the field, cannot do everything. This is particularly true of social work where the process is presently squeezed into two years, and where there are many different routes to qualification, some as post-graduate level, some via employment schemes which resemble apprenticeships. There are now plans to harmonise (the fourth attempt by our calculations) entry and exit criteria. Let us hope that after years of rather unconsidered interference by politicians and by quangos (CCETSW) this settles the matter of who is eligible for training, and what should they know and be able to do when they leave it. 'A triumph of hope over experience' (as Dr Johnson once described second marriages) perhaps, but a hope nonetheless.

Turning now to the questionnaire results pertinent to the issue of what it would be reasonable for professional-grade staff to know, we have had some troubling findings to report particularly regarding knowledge of outcome research. There are various places from which staff could have obtained answers to our test questions: from qualifying and post-qualification training, from supervision experiences, from colleagues, and so forth. Indeed, though we asked staff to complete the questionnaire without conferring, we had no control over compliance. Thus the 'phone a friend', 'ask the local audience', and 'look it up' opportunities were potentially in place, but still the figures on correct nominations remained very low, leading us to conclude that this sort of knowledge is just not in the professional culture.

Reactions to the presentation of these figures (on knowledge of effectiveness research) at conferences produces two sharply different reactions according to audience make-up. Practitioners simply request that the situation be remedied via the CEBSS project, and this is what we have done. If the problem in the first instance is simple lack of information, then provide it. When we have done so, the course evaluation figures have been extremely positive; the commonest qualitative comment being variants of 'nice to be *taught* something for a change'. At conferences and seminars for social care academics though, there is much straightforward interest, other reactions have regularly occurred, including lengthy debates on 'what is evidence', which we in the social care field have too long postponed. This is because it often causes academics to become tired and emotional since they anticipate a debate without an apparent end and one which distracts them from the bread and butter issues of providing training within CCETSW's Rorschachian requirements.

Our response at CEBSS has been to take on this debate anyway and to provide as many practical examples as possible, of what evidence-based training implies. We have also produced two discussion papers, *Research and Practice in Social Care: Mind the Gap* (Sheldon and Macdonald, 1999) and *Changing One's Mind, the Final Frontier* (Macdonald and Sheldon, 1998). These have produced lively exchanges which have prompted us to provide Critical Appraisal Skills training to social care tutors, including an element on criteria for evaluating qualitative research.

Another reaction has typically taken the form of an argument, that to ask staff for distinct information about research (title, the author, description), does not accurately reflect the level of working knowledge that they hold. This seems to be an argument for subliminal conditioning, that is, that staff have absorbed a lot of such knowledge which, though they cannot recall its details, nevertheless, guides their work via a set of professional reflexes. One can only ask whether being 'a natural' in this way would be acceptable if the topic were law, or indeed, stopping distances in the wet?

The problem is *not* that students, practitioners or service managers regard an early concentration in training on questions of the quality of evidence as esoteric or distracting from practical issues. These groups when offered remedial training, vote with their feet; the Directors of Social Services vote with their wallets. The problem is rather that there is insufficient expertise and insufficient time on crowded timetables. There are, unfortunately, some perverse disincentives to following this course of action, which we will now review.

Obstacles to Evidence-based Training

As we have seen, service-effectiveness research often comes to the 'wrong' conclusions. Who would have thought that care-management in mental health (a policy to which we have been committed by politicians) would double rather than halve the hospital admission rate (Rose and Marshall, 1975), an outcome which, we know from client-opinion research to be the very one which service-users most ardently desire to avoid (Macdonald and Sheldon, 1998)? Who would have expected that counselling the victims of trauma might actually impede their recovery? (Wessely, Rose and Bisson, 2000). How curmudgeonly does one have to be to predict that extensive support for families with a young member who deliberately poisons or harms themselves would produce no better outcomes than standard out-patient care? (Gibbons et al., 1978).

Changing curricula, putting on new courses, dropping certain elements is both time-consuming, and affects reputations. There is a well-documented tendency in social care to develop 'crushes' on particular ideas, theories and sets of findings (Sheldon, 1978; Sheldon and Macdonald, 1999). Such emotional attachments offer a semblance of security in a rapidly changing world; are incorporated into course mission statements and become badges of identity for staff. Everyone does this, it is part of the human condition, but there are personal and organisational precautions which can and should be taken against such tendencies, when the welfare of others depends upon our capacity to embrace new, or old, ideas based on better evidence. It is a technical, but also an ethical issue and what we, the less alienated and up against it, expect when we use public services. Interestingly, if at dissemination conferences we ask staff to design a research study to establish the effectiveness of brain surgery for mental disorder, or of ECT, they always come up with the very strictest forms of randomised controlled trial, with the procedures in the hands of a public notary largely because they disapprove of such interventions. When designing studies for social care, however, they are worryingly relaxed about the need for such methodological precautions.

The next obstacle is curriculum development and how it occurs. An ideal situation, though not so ideal as to be unknown, is for a committee comprising staff, students, practice teachers and local social services managers to meet regularly to review course streams against anonymous evaluations from students, and to look at how far their content reflects current best evidence. This kind of 'feedback loop' involves all stakeholders in the quality evaluation process. Such arrangements exist on some courses in full force, but on many only as annual 'how was it for you?' meetings. They could instead be required as basic, good practice on all.

What is taught, particularly regarding research and theory, varies greatly, and is often still (Sheldon, 1978) only loosely connected to the practice curriculum

(Marsh and Tresiliotis, 1996). Thus the range and coverage of course streams and modules more often reflects staff interests and knowledge (since buying in other expertise is expensive) and a virtue is made of existing resources.

An associated problem is that since we lack agreed methodological criteria against which to evaluate course elements, there is an inflationary pressure within curricula created by new and promising material coming in (all too slowly in our experience) at the front end, and little or nothing being discarded as a matter of explicit decision at the back end. More often, someone with a given expertise leaves, someone with a rather different expertise is appointed, and given the smallness of most staff groups, the scope for additional mugging up is limited. There are 14 course providers in our region, some large, some quite small, some teach developmental psychology to their students, several do not; they are all approved by CCETSW. One must ask, how are students to make proper assessments of needs if they are not equipped with a template of normal, average, typical physical, psychological and social development? The point is, that such matters are rarely a matter of considered *choice*. Many other things will be taught, which may not be taught elsewhere. Diversity? Richness? Proper academic freedom? Such matters are more to do with such things, we suspect, as short-term survival, comfort, inertia, underfunding, and sometimes, perhaps, a lack of imagination about who from partnerships could teach what, and for how much?

Let us end this part of the discussion with a quotation from an educationalist writing forty years ago about the need for an 'evolutionary approach' to curriculum development:

> *Applied practice and scientific knowledge are seen here as the resultant of a cumulation of selectively retained tentatives, remaining from the hosts that have been weeded out by experience. Such a perspective leads to a considerable respect for tradition in teaching practice.*
>
> (Campbell 1959, in Campbell and Stanley, 1963)

There is now a 'Campbell Collaboration' a new 'sister' organisation of the Cochrane Collaboration which researches the Health and Social Care field, dedicated to evidence-based social policy and social interventions. (More details at the end of this book.)

To sum up the staff to student ratios in universities in general, but in the social care discipline in particular, now threaten effective professional training. Lots of links, networks, discussion groups, and training packs will simply not do in place of research-informed teaching delivered by a field expert. We can think of few other subjects than 'what is known from effectiveness about what we are training you to do' that, even if resources are short, should nevertheless remain a top priority.

A further obstacle to evidence-based curriculum development has loomed up over the last ten or so years. It is, one of us is saddened to say, a corruption of the principles of behaviourism. Its poorly thought out principles state that all training and education must have a visible behavioural outcome, though who is going to be there to watch for it is an interesting question. 'Learning outcomes', beloved of social services training departments, whose staff privately think them silly but publicly insist on them, disfavour events which merely seek to educate. Nevertheless, knowledge, for example, of the nature and development of personal and social problems, or of what are the most promising policy and social intervention options, can track through to skills and professional behaviour, though not always directly, and not always quickly. There is surely room for both education and training at pre- and post-qualifying level, each feeding the other? However, at present, robust, didactic, theoretical and research-based teaching is being disfavoured because it is not in line with the principles of 'adult learning', which from our experience and examination of the literature equates with treating adults as if they were intellectually impaired children.

Our observations lead us to believe that exactly the opposite is true. Staff are *hungry* for information based on good evidence of how to do their jobs better. The CEBSS project can fill lecture theatres three to five times over for any event which seeks to provide such teaching.

These distorting factors are, unfortunately, typical of the social care field. Training, whether at qualifying or post-qualification level was once very vaguely organised and unsure of its aims, so, now it proceeds, after due criticism, in the opposite direction, and then overshoots. Here is an extreme example of the present position, which originates, contra-stereotype, from one of our older provincial universities and is a leaked memorandum of guidance for academic staff who have to compile course guidelines:

> In a two page memo on how to write descriptions of courses under the illuminating heading 'writing aims and learning outcomes for module specifications' lecturers are advised to avoid certain words and phrases 'because they are too difficult to quantify'. The offending terms include; 'know', 'understand', 'obtain a working knowledge of', 'have a good grasp of', 'be familiar with', and 'learn the basics of'. Only words like 'appraise', 'formulate', 'conceptualise', 'initiate', and 'synthesise' should be used.
>
> (*Private Eye*, 1008, 11.8.2000)

The new General Social Care Council and its attendant training organisation must take note of these issues. They are, after all, a central feature of all recent guidelines and service frameworks emerging from government. But, surely, there is scope here for those leaders of the social care professions to take a positive lead regarding the issues of evidence-based service-provision, and not merely to do what they must? The expertise is there, but at present, it is not being effectively drawn upon at a national level.

Recommendations

Professional training courses should begin with a sequence on this history of social welfare; the 'learning outcome', should be the acquisition of a sense of 'place'; or, as the old town plan displays used to indicate, 'You are here'.

Prior to coming on a course students (most of whom ask for preparatory reading) should be directed to texts on how to evaluate arguments. We can think of no better recommendation than Gilovich's *How We Know What Isn't So: The Fallibility of Reason in Everyday Life* (1991) and Leonard Gibbs' and Eileen Gambrill's book on critical thinking (Gibbs and Gambrill, 1996). This is just to introduce the idea that a career in social care requires intellectual skills as well as an emotional commitment.

This preparatory work in place, there should be a course in critical thinking skills, in other words, a sequence on evaluating the evidence which will be presented on the rest of the programme. There is some empirical research to suggest that this teaching changes the way students look at all subsequent propositions put to them (Macdonald and Sheldon, 1998), including some that suggests that social science training of this type improves evaluative skills in physical sciences students, compared to what they normally get (Gilovich, 1991).

Next should follow courses in Applied Sociology and Social Policy, but with an emphasis on what might be called *social epidemiology*, that is, on the origins and prevalence of social problems and what we know of their development and effects. In other words:

- how many children are brought into care each year, and from what backgrounds?
- what happens to them when they leave care?
- is there a clear association between unemployment and suicide?
- what is the prevalence of mental illness in Britain, how secure are the figures and what social and other factors exacerbate and limit its effects?
- what are the figures on juvenile crime, from what backgrounds do persistent offenders come; what is the association with social class and different types of upbringing?

And so forth. Such courses are the social care equivalent of epidemiology and public health courses in medicine. They should not be purely theoretical, as they often are, if the subject is taught at all that is; they should be based on empirical research, of which there is a wealth.

Informing Policy-makers About Evidence

One of the aims of the CEBSS project is to influence elected members. A daunting idea in prospect, but, after five conferences where the aims of evidence-based social services have been debated with them, surprisingly easy. In short, when they have the ideas explained to them with suitable practical examples, they buy it: at least in our experience. The common focus of debate is 'what could we do to improve services without additional cost?' The answer which CEBSS (surprisingly) provides, since there isn't supposed to be one, is to back senior managers regarding properly considered, but not entirely foreseeable risks, so that they can then extend this policy to their front-line staff. Apprehensions of risk, largely based on dramatic single cases which are very untypical of the national picture of safety, particularly in the child care and community care fields, distort the priorities of social services departments, focusing the attention of staff on keeping all-inclusive case-records up-to-date in case there is an accident, rather than on benign, non-statutory, preventative social work service which is, in fact more likely to reduce risk over all, than 'full metal jacket', 'heavy end' (as social services staff call it) interventions. The focus of the work of the CEBSS project in this regard is to persuade elected members of the following:

- That risk-factor schedules, though always seen as the answer to preventing future tragedies in child care and mental health are not necessarily reliable.
- That dramatic, or local, single cases of apparent service-failure are not a secure guide to policy development.
- That many enquiry reports, which have an undue influence on policy both nationally and locally are riddled with recommendations based on hindsight.

Here are the sanest views we know regarding this problem, beginning with a quote from the Inquiry panel into the death of Jasmine Beckford, and ending with an analysis of exactly how much logic is present:

We are entitled to judge a person's actions by reference to what was and should, reasonably, have been in his or her mind at the relevant time. We are not entitled to blame him or her for not knowing, or foreseeing what a reasonable person would neither have known or foreseen. In assessing whether a reasonable person would have known or foreseen an event, we are entitled to have regard to what actually happened, though, of course, the fact that an event occurred does not mean that a reasonable person would necessarily have known that it would occur or would have foreseen its occurrence. But that fact that it did occur (and was not an Act of God but the result of human action or inaction) gives rise to a presumption—either that there was knowledge that it would occur, or that foresight would have indicated its likely occurrence.

(London Borough of Brent, 1985: p32).

The logic of the last sentence can be reviewed in the light of a less emotive subject. Our son is, by common consent (he is small of stature and his heart is elsewhere), exceedingly unlikely to score a try in rugby. Today he returns covered in mud and glory, having scored. The authors of the report would not tell us: ' the fact that the try did occur (and was not the act of God but the result of human action or inaction) gives rise to a presumption—either that there was knowledge that it would occur, or that foresight would have indicated its likely occurrence'. Surely not. It happened; but remains unlikely.

(Macdonald and Macdonald, 2000).

The point is that, contrary to early views, local policy-makers enjoy being brought in on these debates, and express at least a verbal willingness to ensure that considered risks, even if they go wrong, will not result in witch hunts. Time will tell.

Access to Research

This was seen as a priority by staff responding to our questionnaire but these conclusions can be brief because we feel, surveying the developments in Health, and to a lesser extent in Social Care, that electronic media will solve this problem over the next five years or so. Plans are in place for an Electronic Library for Social Care. Leaving aside our own modest contribution in CEBSS the Cochrane Collaboration, the Campbell Collaboration and the University of York Centre for Reviews and Dissemination are pumping out systematic reviews with attendant recommendations for policy and practice relevant to the Social Care field. This seems to be an unstoppable process, which is bound to influence policy-making, management and practice, providing that there are people with knowledge of these trends to debate the issues with staff face-to-face, and to work to establish the day-to-day practicalities of evidence-based services provision within departments, where there is considerable enthusiasm (as this questionnaire exercise shows) on which to capitalise.

The answer to this problem of access is provided by research reviews. They are becoming, as indicated, more and more systematic. That is, authors are pre-establishing their problem area with greater specificity, pre-publishing their search terms and inclusion and exclusion criteria, and in some cases, their methodological ones.

The CEBSS has published four research reviews:

- *New Directions: Day Services for People with Learning Disabilities in the 1990s*; Simons and Watson, 1999
- *Occupational Therapy in Social Services Departments*; Mountain, 2000
- *Quality of Life for People with Learning Disabilities in Supported Housing in the Community*; Felce, 2000

- *Home Care: A Review of Effectiveness and Outcomes.*Godfrey et al., 2000

and makes others available. However, the matter is not left there; for every review, of which free copies are supplied to our consortium, we conduct a series of day conferences on implications for policy, management and practice to all layers within departments.

Creating and Sustaining an Evidence-based Culture

A key finding in the questionnaire results is that staff feel that they are given limited support from management for the task of incorporating research findings into their practice. Having completed a long series of conferences on available evidence (both general trends and client group specific ones) we are still left with the problem, well revealed in the evidence-based health care field (CRD, 1999) that explanation, exhortation, training and the distribution of selected literature alone, will not necessarily change workplace behaviour. The additional requirement is for reinforcement from colleagues and management. Indeed the evidence on dissemination effectiveness closely mirrors that of social work effectiveness research itself, namely that the gap between clients being given new information, insight and understanding, and translating this into behavioural change is very easy to underestimate.

Our approach to this problem is to put on dissemination events to which preselected teams of staff, representing the different layers of responsibility within departments, are invited together to conferences and meetings; later they report back on obstacles and progress with the aims they decided upon as part of this training.

Almost every department in the CEBSS consortium now has an 'evidence-based services strategy document', against which progress of a plan is regularly monitored within the project. Ready access to Directors and other senior managers helps in this regard.

There is one further development worthy of mention. Without prompting, staff from half of our participating departments have set up their own evidence-based social services groups (CEBSS, 1999). These meet regularly at lunchtimes and out of hours, or on specified training days and invite expert speakers from both within and outside the departments. Given what we have learned from this research about practical obstacles to evidence-based working, this is commitment indeed.

Some challenging findings have been thrown up by this research, some predictable, some much less so, but at least we now have a data-base against which to measure progress towards the ideal already set out.

There was some resistance to the questionnaire exercise in the early stages of the CEBSS project. Action, rather than measurement, was seen as the priority, which advice was usually accompanied by military metaphors, such as the need to 'hit the ground running'. Our counter response was that it would be more sensible to take some aerial photographs of the ground first and plan accordingly (Dixon, 1976, for a surprisingly relevant text on military disasters).

On the basis of our three years experience in the CEBSS project, with government at national and local level picking up on this issue with increasing enthusiasm, we now look forward to a point, about ten years away, when the term evidence-based can be dropped, since it will be an automatic and well-funded assumption, that, *of course*, public services are based on current best evidence.

UNIVERSITY
of
EXETER

CENTRE FOR EVIDENCE-BASED SOCIAL SERVICES

QUESTIONNAIRE
ON THE USE OF RESEARCH BY
SOCIAL SERVICES STAFF

- ### Background and Purpose

- The Department of Health and the Social Services Departments of the South and South West of England have jointly funded a Centre for Evidence-based Social Services at the University of Exeter. This has five major functions:
  - (i)   to disseminate in as 'user friendly' a way as possible the results and implications of existing research both on the origins and development of social problems and on the effectiveness of different approaches to them;
  - (ii) to provide training in interpreting and using research findings to inform practice;
  - (iii) to offer advice informed by research to managers and policy makers;
  - (iv) to carry out or commission studies in areas where there are significant gaps in knowledge; and
  - (v)   to work in co-operation with representative bodies for service-users and carers.

- In order to develop our programme of work we need your help, firstly to get a 'baseline' measure of the existing use of research in Departments, and secondly to gather your views on the priorities for both dissemination and future research in your area.

- We hope that you will share our excitement over this project, which is essentially about improving services by offering greater professional support to staff. This survey is *entirely confidential* and no individual will be identifiable from the report produced.

Background Information

1. Gender   (please tick)

    Male   ○

    Female   ○

2. Age (please write in)   _____ years

3. Years in Social Services employment (please write in)_____ years

4. Ethnicity (please write in)

5. Do you hold any of the following professional qualifications?   (please tick)

    DipSW   ○

    CQSW   ○

    CSS   ○

    DipCOT   ○

    Other (please specify)   ○

6. Do you hold any of the following academic qualifications?   (please tick)

    PhD   ○

    Masters Degree   ○

    Bachelors Degree   ○

    Diploma/Certificate ○

    Other (please specify) ○

7. Are you a member of a professional organisation?   (please tick)

    Yes   ○

    No   ○

    If *yes*, please write in its name: _____

8. What is the title of your post? (please write in)   _____

9. Are you in the field or residential or day care work?   (please tick)

    Field   ○

    Residential   ○

    Day Care   ○

    Other (please specify) ○

10. With which client-group(s) do you mainly work?   (please tick)

    Elderly   ○

    Chronically sick/Disabled ○

    Learning Disability   ○

    Children and Families ○

    Youth Justice   ○

    Mentally Ill   ○

    Medical   ○

    Other (please specify) ○

Departmental Influences on Use of Research

11. Do you have opportunities to consult either a line-manager or a designated supervisor about your work? (please tick)

Yes, weekly by appointment	O
Yes, fortnightly by appointment	O
Yes, monthly by appointment	O
Yes, by appointment but less frequently	O
Yes, but ad-hoc opportunities only	O
No, I do not have such opportunities	O

12. What is your opinion of the quality of the consultation/supervision opportunities available to you? (please tick)

Very satisfactory	O
Quite satisfactory	O
Unsatisfactory	O
Very unsatisfactory	O

Briefly state your reasons for your choice of answer (please write in)

13. Are research findings (either on the development of social problems or on interventions) much discussed in consultation/supervision meetings? (please tick)

Often	O
Sometimes	O
Hardly ever	O
Never	O

14. Are research findings much discussed at team or other departmental meetings? (please tick)

Often	O
Sometimes	O
Hardly ever	O
Never	O

15. How many departmental training courses have you attended in the last two years?

(please write in) _____

If you have attended any training courses, were any of them to do with

(i) interpreting research findings (please tick)

Yes	O
No	O
Not sure	O

(ii) using research findings in your work? (please tick)

Yes	O
No	O
Not sure	O

16. To what extent do you feel that your Department encourages you to keep abreast of the
    research literature relevant to your job?   (please tick)

Gives a lot of encouragement	O
Gives some encouragement	O
Gives a little encouragement	O
Gives no encouragement at all	O
Discourages	O

17. Are any of the following facilities available to you within your Department to help you
    to keep abreast of research findings? If so, how satisfied are you with these services/
    facilities?   (please tick)

Facilities	Yes, very satisfactory	Yes, quite satisfactory	Yes, but unsatisfactory	No, do not have	I am not sure
Library	O	O	O	O	O
Circulated journals	O	O	O	O	O
Research summaries	O	O	O	O	O
Abstracts services	O	O	O	O	O
Discussion groups	O	O	O	O	O
Research Presentations	O	O	O	O	O
Computer databases	O	O	O	O	O
Other (please specify):					

Please list any particular sources of satisfaction or dissatisfaction:

18. Please summarise below what your department could do further to encourage the use of
    research findings. (please write in)

19. How far do you see the task of keeping abreast of research trends as
    (i) a personal, professional responsibility? (please mark the point on the scale which best represents your view)

A personal, professional responsibility						Not a personal, professional responsibility

└──────┴────────┴────────┴────────┴────────┴────────┴──────┘

(ii) a departmental responsibility? (please mark the point on the scale which best represents your view)

A departmental responsibility						Not a departmental responsibility

└──────┴────────┴────────┴────────┴────────┴────────┴──────┘

Opportunities for Professional Reading

20. Do you subscribe to, or have regular access to publications relevant to your job?

(please tick)

Yes ○
No ○

If *yes*, please write in the titles:

21. Which of the following types of publication are you most likely to read? (please tick)

Types of publication	Very likely to read it	Quite likely to read it	Rather unlikely to read it	Very unlikely to read it	I am not sure
Practice journal	○	○	○	○	○
Academic journal	○	○	○	○	○
A relevant magazine	○	○	○	○	○
Internal policy documents	○	○	○	○	○
Internal research publications	○	○	○	○	○
Research reviews	○	○	○	○	○
Government publications	○	○	○	○	○
Books on social work in general	○	○	○	○	○
Books on your own specialist interest	○	○	○	○	○
Publications about statutory responsibilities	○	○	○	○	○
Other (please specify):					

22. When were you last able to read (rather than glance at) any literature pertinent to your job?

    (please tick)

This week	O
Last week	O
2–3 weeks ago	O
1 month ago	O
Over 6 months go	O
Over 1 year ago	O
Too long to remember	O

23. Where does any such reading take place?

    (please tick)

Mostly at work	O
Mostly at home	O
Equally at home and work	O
Other (please specify)	O
Not applicable	O

24. There are many reasons why professionals find it difficult to keep abreast of the professional literature. How important are each of the following reasons in limiting your reading? (please tick)

Reasons	Very important	Quite important	Not so important	Definitely not important
time pressures of work in general	O	O	O	O
access to literature	O	O	O	O
cost of journals/books	O	O	O	O
family commitments	O	O	O	O
lack of knowledge of what to read and how to interpret it	O	O	O	O
no support for this in my workplace	O	O	O	O
reading research is not necessary in my job	O	O	O	O

Appraising Research Findings

25. Have you read any evaluative research (studies testing out the effectiveness of an approach or services) relevant to your field?

    (please tick)

Yes	O
No	O
Not sure	O

    If *yes* please identify a study that has been influential? (please write in title or author(s)):

26. How did this first come to your attention?   (please tick)
        Learnt about it as a student on a qualifying course   O
        Learnt about it on post-qualification training course   O
        Came across it by chance   O
        Recommended in departmental circular   O
        Recommended to me by a colleague   O
        Recommended by librarian   O
        Regularly read the publication in which it was contained   O
        Other (please specify)   O

_____

        Not applicable   O

The next few questions are designed to establish your current knowledge of research methods *(this is not an exam—just means to assess current understanding—no conferring or looking anything up please!)*

27. Have you ever come across a published client-opinion study?   (please tick)
                        Yes   O
                        No   O
                        Not sure   O
    If *yes*, can you recall the title of such a study or its author(s)? (please write in)

28. What factors other than professional interventions might account for a positive change reported in a client-opinion study? (please write in):

29. Do you know of any randomised-controlled trials of social work interventions (that is study where subjects are randomly allocated to 2 or more conditions for comparison purposes)?   (please tick)
                        Yes   O
                        No   O
                        Not sure   O
    If *yes*, can you recall the the title of such a study or its author(s)? (please write in)

30. You may have come across references to statistical significance in articles that you have read, do you know what this term means?   (please tick)
                        Yes   O
                        No   O
                        Not sure   O
    If *yes*, please explain briefly what it means? (please write in):

31. How would you assess your current ability critically to appraise a research article
relevant to your field?   (please tick)

Very confident	O
Quite confident	O
Not very confident	O
Not at all confident	O

Relevance of Research to Professional Practice

32. How relevant would you say research is to your job?   (please tick)

Very relevant	O
Quite relevant	O
Not very relevant	O
Not at all relevant	O

33. To what extent do you think that research findings actually inform your own day-to-day
practice?   (please tick)

All the time	O
Quite often	O
Rarely	O
Not at all	O

34. In what ways do you think reading more research publications might influence your
practice? Please select the item which you think best represents you view. (please tick)

Greater knowledge of the *nature* of social problems   O
might help me make better assessments of need

Greater knowledge of *helping methods or approaches*   O
would assist me in selecting one more likely to be effective

Not sure that additional reading would   O
make any difference to what I do

35. Do you think that if you could have access to more research literature that your practice
would improve?   (please tick)

Definitely	O
Maybe	O
Already read enough	O
Definitely not	O

36. Can you think of a way in which your practice has been changed as a result of reading a
research article or book?   (please tick)

Yes	O
No	O
Not sure	O

If *yes*, please briefly explain how your practice changed (please write in):

Expectations of the Centre for Evidence-based Social Services

37. Below is a list of activities that the Centre for Evidence-based Social Services will be involved in in the future. Please indicate how important each of these activities might be for your professional practice. (please read through and then tick as appropriate)

Activities	Very important	Quite important	Not very important	Definitely not important	Not sure
General training on the concept of evidence-based approaches	O	O	O	O	O
Training in specific approaches which have a good research track record	O	O	O	O	O
Help to gain better access to research material	O	O	O	O	O
Publishing research reviews and summaries with practice implications spelt out	O	O	O	O	O
Filling gaps in available research	O	O	O	O	O
Advising management	O	O	O	O	O
Setting up electronic data-bases of findings	O	O	O	O	O
Training in research methodology and how to interpret studies	O	O	O	O	O
Advising training departments on current research	O	O	O	O	O
Advising local policy-makers on current research trends	O	O	O	O	O
Encouraging local research and evaluation exercises	O	O	O	O	O
Holding periodic conferences on research trends	O	O	O	O	O
Working with local librarians on information needs in Social Services	O	O	O	O	O
Training Team Leaders	O	O	O	O	O
Training other supervisors or mentors	O	O	O	O	O
Working with DipSW and other professional course staff	O	O	O	O	O
Working with users and carers groups	O	O	O	O	O
Training local dissemination personnel	O	O	O	O	O
Other (please specify):					

38. What is your reaction to the idea of a greater emphasis being placed on research evidence in planning and delivering social services? (please tick)

A good idea and long overdue ○
Welcome the idea but have some misgivings ○
Nothing new, why all the fuss ○
Don't like the idea ○

If you have doubts or misgivings, please explain what they are. (write in)

39. Of the problems that you encounter in your work (either those experienced or posed by clients, or those which come from your organisation) which do you think are in most need of further research? (please write in up to 3 in order of importance)

40. What is your opinion of the project's chances of success in producing a greater emphasis on evidence-based approaches in your Department? (please tick)

Every chance of success ○
A good chance of success ○
A fifty/fifty chance of success ○
A low chance of success ○
No chance of success ○

Briefly state your reasons for your choice of answer. (please write in)

41. What do you think are the most important obstacles to developing evidence-based approaches in your department or the main reasons why such an objective might be misguided? Please select up to *four* items from the menu below and number from 1 to 4 in order of importance (with 1 as first priority, 2 as second, etc.).

Main obstacles to be over come	Please rank order (from 1 to 4)
Pressure of work in department	
Lack of knowledge of research	
Fashions come and fashions go, so will this one	
Lack of management support	
Academic results are one thing, the realities of practice another	
Distrust of 'narrow scientific' approaches	
Lack of back-up facilities	
Government and Departmental policies leave little room for innovation	
I can't cope with any more change	
Funding constraints	
Low staff morale	
Inadequate qualifying training in interpreting research	
Social work owes more to art than to science	
I think there is a hidden agenda (please give us your views)	
Other (please specify):	

Have you any other comments to make or advice to give regarding this project? (please write in)

Thank you for spending time to complete this questionnaire. A report on our findings will be made available to you as soon as the results have been analysed.

Please return your questionnaire as soon as possible to:

Professor Brian Sheldon
Centre for Evidence-based Social Services
Amory Building
University of Exeter
Exeter EX4 4RJ

Contact Details

Joan McCord (Crime and Justice Review Group), Professor, Temple University. Tel: +1 610 667 6197 or +1 215 204 8080; Fax: +1 610 667 0568; E-mail: mccord@vm.temple.edu

Haluk Soydan (Social Work/Social Welfare Review Group), Research Director, CUS, The National Board of Health and Welfare, S-106 30 Stockholm, Sweden. Tel: +46 8 5555 34 41 (mob: +46 70 537 96 86); Fax: +46 8 5555 32 24; E-mail: Haluk.Soydan@sos.se; website address: http://campbell.gse.upenn.edu/

Geraldine Macdonald, University of Bristol. Tel: 0117 954 6718; Fax: 0117 954 6748; E-mail: geraldine.macdonald@bristol.ac.uk

Centre for Evidence-based Studies, University of Exeter. Tel: 01392 262 865; Fax: 01392 262 858; E-mail s.e.boseley@exeter.ac.uk

References

Adams, R., Dominelli, L., and Payne, M. (Eds.) (1998). *Social Work Themes, Issues and Critical Debates*. Basingstoke: Macmillan.

Appleby, L. (1992). Suicide in Psychiatric Patients: Risk and Prevention. *British Journal of Psychiatry*, 161: pp749–758.

Appleby, L. (1997). *National Confidential Inquiry into Suicides and Homicides by People with Mental Illness*. London: Department of Health.

Bacon, F. (1620). Norum Organnus Scientarum II Aphorism VI. Harmondsworth (1998): Penguin Edition.

Birch Committee. *Manpower in the Social Services*. London: HMSO.

Brewer, C., and Lait, J.C. (1980). *Can Social Work Survive?* London: Temple Smith.

British Association of Social Workers (1975). *The Code of Ethics for Social Work*. Birmingham: BASW.

Brown, M.J., and McCulloch, J.W. (1975). *A Study of the Reading Habits of Social Workers*. University of Birmingham, Clearing House for Social Services Research.

Butler Sloss, E. (1988). *Report of the Inquiry into Child Abuse in Cleveland 1987*, Cmd. 412. London: HMSO.

Byford, S., Harrington, R., Torgeson, D., Kerfoot, M., Dyer, E., Harrington, V., Woodham, A., Gill, J., and McNiven, F. (1999). Cost-effectiveness Analysis of a Home-based Social Work Intervention for Children and Adolescents Who Have Deliberately Poisoned Themselves: Results of a Randomised Controlled Trial. *British Journal of Psychiatry*, 174: pp56–62.

Cabot, R.C. (1931). Treatment in Social Casework and the Need for Tests of its Success and Failure, *Proceedings of the National Conference of Social Work*.

Campbell, D.T., and Stanley, J.C. (1963). *Experimental and Quasi-experimental Designs for Research*. Boston: Houghton Mifflin Company.

Care Standards Act 2000. The Stationery Office.

CASP (1999). *Critical Appraisal Skills Report*. University of Exeter, Centre for Evidence-based Social Services.

CEBSS (Centre for Evidence-based Social Services) (1999) *Annual Report*. University of Exeter.

CEBSS (Centre for Evidence-based Social Services) (2000) *Annual Report*. University of Exeter.

Centre for Reviews and Dissemination (CRD) (1999). Getting Evidence into Practice. *Effective Healthcare Bulletin*, 5(1).

Cochrane, A.L. (1973). *Effectiveness and Efficiency: Random Reflections on Health Services.* London: Nuffield Provincial Hospitals Trust.

Cohen, J.A., and Mannarino, A.P. (1996). A Treatment Outcome Study for Sexually Abused Pre-school Children: Initial Findings. *Journal of American Academy of Child and Adolescent Psychiatry*, 35: pp42–50.

Dalrymple, J. (1994). Devil's Island: What Really Happened on the Orkneys. *Sunday Times*, 27th February

Daniels, M., and Hill, H.B. (1952). Chemotherapy of Pulmonary Tuberculosis in Young Adults: An Analysis of Three Medical Research Council Trials. *British Medical Journal*, 1(1162).

Davies, M. (2000). *The Blackwell Encyclopaedia of Social Work.* Oxford: Blackwell.

Dennett, D.C. (1991). *Consciousness Explained.* London: Allan Lane.

Department of Health (1994). *A Wider Strategy for Research in the Personal Social Services.* London: HMSO.

Dixon, N. (1976). *On the Psychology of Military Incompetence.* London: Jonathan Cape.

Felce, D. (2000). *Quality of Life for People with Learning Disabilities in Supported Housing in the Community: A Review of Research.* Exeter University, Centre for Evidence-Based Social Services.

Fischer, J. (1973). Is Casework Effective?: A Review. *Social Work*, 1: pp107–110.

Fischer, J. (1976). *The Effectiveness of Social Casework.* Springfield, IL: Charles C. Thomas.

Fischer, J., and Corcoran, K. (1994). *Measures for Clinical Practice* (Vols I & II). New York: Free Press.

Fisher, M. (Ed.) (1983). *Speaking of Clients.* Social Services Monographs: Research in Practice. Joint Unit for Social Services Research, University of Sheffield.

Fisher, M., Newton, C., and Sainsbury, E. (1984). *Mental Health Social Work Observed.* London: George Allen and Unwin.

Gibbons, J.S., et al. (1978). Evaluation of a Social Work Service for Self-poisoning Patients. *British Journal of Psychiatry*, 133: pp111–118.

Gibbs, L., and Gambrill, E. (1996). *Critical Thinking for Social Workers: A Workbook.* London: Pine Forge Press.

Gilovich, T. (1991). *How We Know What Isn't So: The Fallibility of Human Reason in Everyday Life.* New York: The Free Press.

Godfrey, M., Randall, T., Long, A., Grant, M. (2000). *Home Care: A Review of Effectiveness and Outcomes.* University of Exeter, Centre for Evidence-based Social Services.

Grady, K.E., and Wallston, B.S. (1988). Research in Health Care Settings. *Applied Social Research Methods Series*, Vol. 14. London: Sage.

Greene, J., and D'Oliveira, M. (1989). *Learning to use Statistical Tests in Psychology.* Milton Keynes: Open University Press.

Griffiths Report (1988). *Community Care: Agenda for Action.* London: HMSO.

Grinnell, R.M. (1981). *Social Work Research and Evaluation.* Illinois: FE Peacock Publishers Inc.

Herbert, M. (1990). *Planning a Research Project: A Guide for Practitioners and Trainers in the Helping Professions.* London: Gaskell.

Howitt, D. (1992). *Child Abuse Errors: When Good Intentions Go Wrong.* Hertfordshire: Harvester Wheatsheaf.

Jones, W.C. and Borgatta, E.F. (1972) Methodology of Evaluation. In Mullen, E.J., and Dumpson (Eds.) *Evaluation of Social Intervention.* San Francisco, CA: Jossey-Bass.

Leff, J. (Ed.) (1997). *Care in the Community: Illusion or Reality?* Chichester: Wiley.

Lehrman, L.J. (1949). Success and Failure of Treatment of Children in Child Guidance Clinics of the Jewish Board of Guardians. *Research Monographs*, 1.

Local Government Management Board (LGMB)/Association of Directors of Social Services (ADSS) (1998). *Social Services Workforce Analysis Main Report 1997 Survey.* Report No. 24, Social Services Workforce Series. London: LGMB.

Local Government Management Board (LGMB)/Central Council for Education and Training in Social Work (CCETSW) (1997). *Human Resources for Personal Social Services: From Personnel Administration to Human Resources Management.* London: LGMB.

Lomax, T., and Younger-Ross, S. (1998). Outlands, Five Years On. *Community Care Management*, 6(1): pp37–40.

London Borough of Brent (1985). *A Child in Trust: The Report of the Panal of Inquiry into the Circumstances Surrounding the Death of Jasmine Bedford.* London Borough of Brent.

London Borough of Greenwich (1987). *A Child in Mind: The Report of the Commission of Inquiry into the Circumstances Surrounding the Death of Kimberley Carlisle.* London Borough of Greenwich.

Macdonald, G.M., with Winkley, A. (1999). *What Works in Child Protection?* Essex: Barnardo's.

Macdonald, G.M., and Sheldon, B. (1992). Contemporary Studies of the Effectiveness of Social Work. *British Journal of Social Work*, 22(6): pp615–643.

Macdonald, G.M., and Sheldon, B. (1998). Community Care for the Mentally Ill: Consumers' Views. *International Journal of Social Psychiatry*, 43(1): pp35–55.

Macdonald, G.M., and Sheldon, B. (1998). Changing One's Mind: The Final Frontier? *Issues in Social Work Education*, 18(1): pp3–25.

Macdonald, K.I., and Macdonald G.M. (2000). Perceptions of Risk. In Parslow, P. (Ed.). *Risk Assessment in Social Care.* Research Highlights 36. Jessica Kingsley.

Marsh, P., and Triseliotis, J. (1996). *Ready to Practise? Social Workers and Probation Officers: Their Training and Their First Year of Work.* Aldershot: Avebury.

Marshall, M., and Lockwood, A. (2000). Assertive Community Treatment for People with Severe Mental Disorders (Cochrane Review). In *The Cochrane Library*, Issue 3. Oxford: Update Software.

Marshall, M., Gray, A., Lockwood, A., Green, R. (2000). Case Management for People with

Severe Mental Disorders (Cochrane Review). In *The Cochrane Library*, Issue 3, Oxford: Update Software.

Mayer, J.E, and Timms, N. (1970). *The Client Speaks: Working Class Impressions of Casework.* London: Routledge and Kegan Paul.

Maynard, A., and Chalmers, I. (1997). *Non-random Reflections on Health Services Research.* London: BMJ Publishing Group.

Mitchell, M., and Jolley, J. (1988). *Research Design Explained.* London: Holt, Rinehart and Winston Inc.

Monnette, D.R., Sullivan, T.J., and De Jong, C.R. (1989). *Applied Social Research: Tools for the Human Services* (2nd edn.). London: Holt, Rinehart and Winston, Inc.

Mountain, G. (2000). *Occupational Therapy in Social Services Departments.* University of Exeter, Centre for Evidence-based Social Services/College of Occupational Therapists.

Mullen, E.J., and Dumpson, J.R. (Eds.) (1972). *Evaluation of Social Intervention.* San Francisco, CA: Jossey-Bass.

Oppenheim, A.S. (1992). *Questionnaire Design, Interviewing and Attitude Assessment.* London: Pinter.

Parsloe, P. (Ed.) (2000). *Risk Assessment in Social Care and Social Work.* Research Highlights 36. London: Jessica Kingsley Publishers.

Powers, E., and Witmer, H. (1951). *An Experiment in the Prevention of Delinquency—The Cambridge-Somerville Youth Study.* New York: Columbia University Press.

Powers, G.T., Meenagahn, T.M., and Toomey, B.G. (1985). *Practice Focused Research: Integrating Human Service Practice and Research.* New Jersey: Prentice-Hall Inc.

Private Eye (2000). Issue 1008, 11th August.

Reed, J. (1997). Risk Assessment and Clinical Risk Management: The Lessons from Recent Inquiries. *British Journal of Psychiatry*, 170(suppl. 32): pp4–7.

Rees, S. (1987). *Social Work Face to Face.* London: Edward Arnold.

Reid, W.J., and Hanrahan, P. (1980). The Effectiveness of Social Work: Recent Evidence. In Goldberg, E.M., and Connelly, N. (1980). *Evaluative Research in Social Care.* London: Heineman.

Reid, W.J., and Shyne, A. (1968). *Brief and Extended Casework.* London: Columbia University Press.

Richmond, M.E. (1917). *Social Diagnosis.* New York: Russel Sage Foundation.

Roll, J. (2000). *The Care Standards Bill.* Great Britain: Parliament, House of Commons, Library.

Rose, G., and Marshall, T.M. (1975). *Counselling and Social Work: An Experimental Study.* London: John Wiley.

Royal College of Psychiatrists (1996). *Report of the Confidential Inquiry into Homicide and Suicide by Mentally Ill People.* London: Gaskell.

Sackett, D.L., Rosenberg, W.M., Gray, J.H.M., Haynes, R.B., and Richardson, W.S. (1996). Evidence-based Practice: What it is and What it isn't. *British Medical Journal*, 312(7203): pp71–72.

Seebohm Report (1968). *Report of the Committee on Local Authority and Allied Personal Social Services*, Cmnd. 3703. London: HMSO.

Sheldon, B., and Macdonald, G.M. (1998). Community Care for the Mentally Ill: Carer's Views. *International Journal of Social Psychiatry*, 16(1).

Sheldon, B., and Macdonald, G. (1999). *Research and Practice in Social Care: Mind the Gap.* Centre for Evidence-based Social Services, University of Exeter.

Sheldon, B. (1978). Theory and Practice in Social Work: A Re-examination of a Tenuous Relationship. *British Journal of Social Work*, 8(1): pp1–22.

Sheldon, B. (1980). *The Use of Contracts in Social Work.* Birmingham: British Association of Social Workers.

Sheldon, B. (1986). Social Work Effectiveness Experiments: Review and Implications. *British Journal of Social Work*, 16: pp223–242.

Sheldon, B. (1987a). The Psychology of Incompetence. In Drewry, G., Martin, B., and Sheldon, B. (Eds.). *After Beckford: Essays on Child Abuse.* Egham, Surrey: Royal Holloway and Bedford New College.

Sheldon, B. (1987b). Implementing the Findings of Social Work Effectiveness Research. *British Journal of Social Work*, 17: pp573–586.

Sheldon, B. (1995). *Cognitive-behavioural Therapy: Research, Practice, Philosophy.* London: Routledge.

Simons, K., and Watson, D. (1999). *New Directions: Day Services for People with Learning Disabilities in the 1990s: A Review of the Research.* University of Exeter, Centre for Evidence-Based Social Services.

Stein, J., and Gambrill, E. (1977). Facilitating Decision Making in Foster Care. *Social Services Review*, 51: pp502–511.

Thoburn, J., Lewis, A., and Shemmings, D. (1995). *Paternalism or Partnership? Family Involvement in the Child Protection Process. Studies in Child Protection.* London: HMSO.

Whitaker, D.S., and Archer, J.L. (1989). *Research by Social Workers: Capitalising on Experience*, CCETSW Study 9. London: CCETSW.

Wilson, E.O. (1998). *Consilience: The Unity of Knowledge.* London: Little, Brown and Company.

Author Index

Subject Index